ANGELS. Small golden pi~~~~~~~~~~ ~~~~ ~a figures on coffee tables. *Angels.* Acc~~~~~~~~~~~~~~~~~~~g unmistakable acts. *Angel~~~~~~~~~~~~~~~~~~~n clothing to furniture to testimonies.

How are we to interpret this pher~~~~~~~~~ heavenly kindness? A demonic counterfeit? How can we be sure of the good without indulging in the evil?

David Jeremiah has set out to offer some guidance. What a welcome work from his pen. David has that uncanny ability to be deliberate without being dull. You get the details and you don't get sleepy!

How thankful we are to God that he has turned his skills toward this vital issue of angels. His words will deepen your gratitude for God's messengers in light of God's Word.

—MAX LUCADO
author and pastor
San Antonio

SIMPLY PUT, this is an outstanding book! As one would expect from David Jeremiah, this book reflects a theologian's concern, a pastor's heart, and a Biblicist's accuracy.

But more than anything else, this book reflects the power of the pulpit! It preaches in the best and most honored sense of the word, carrying the reader toward convincing closure, chapter after chapter. In a day of many choices, I would recommend this book as a first—and maybe last—selection on angels.

—DR. BRUCE WILKINSON
New York Times best selling author
Atlanta

WITH ALL the curiosity and excitement over angels these days, David Jeremiah presents a refreshing and encouraging look at what the Bible says about angels. Thank you, David, for drawing me closer to God through this wonderful book.

—DAVE DRAVECKY
author and director of Outreach of Hope
Colorado Springs

Angels

THE STRANGE AND
MYSTERIOUS TRUTH

DR. DAVID JEREMIAH

Angels

THE STRANGE AND
MYSTERIOUS TRUTH

Multnomah® Publishers *Sisters, Oregon*

ANGELS: THE STRANGE AND MYSTERIOUS TRUTH
published by Multnomah Publishers, Inc.

Published in association with the literary agency of Yates and Yates
1100 Town & Country Rd., Suite 1300, Orange, CA 92868
© 1996 by David P. Jeremiah, Trustee of the David P. Jeremiah Family Trust
Previously published as *What the Bible Says about Angels*

International Standard Book Number: 1-59052-702-X
Cover design by The DesignWorks Group, Inc.

Unless otherwise indicated, Scripture quotations are from:
The Holy Bible, New International Version (NIV)
©1973, 1984 by International Bible Society,
used by permission of Zondervan Publishing House
Other Scripture quotations are from:
New American Standard Bible (NASB)
© 1960, 1977 by the Lockman Foundation
The New Testament in Modern English, Revised Edition (Phillips)
© 1958, 1960, 1972 by J. B. Phillips

Multnomah is a trademark of Multnomah Publishers, Inc.,
and is registered in the U.S. Patent and Trademark Office.
The colophon is a trademark of Multnomah Publishers, Inc.
Printed in the United States of America

For information:

MULTNOMAH PUBLISHERS, INC.

601 NORTH LARCH STREET

SISTERS, OREGON 97759

Library of Congress Cataloging-in-Publication Data

Jeremiah, David.
  Angels : the strange and mysterious truth/David Jeremiah. --Rev. ed.
    p.   cm.
  Rev. ed. of: What the Bible says about angels. c1996.
  Includes bibliographical references and index.
  ISBN: 1-59052-702-X
  1. Angels--Biblical teaching. I. Jeremiah, David. What the Bible says about angels. II. Title.
BS680.A48J47 2006
235'.3--dc22   2006017136

06 07 08 09 10 — 16 15 14 13 12

to my wife's mother

ANNIE THOMPSON

CONTENTS

*All glory be
to the God of the angels*

Chapter One

WHAT IN THE WORLD ARE ANGELS DOING?

I N A DOCTOR'S OFFICE one fall day a decade ago, I was told I had cancer. I'm sure you'll understand when I say I was fearful. It was one of those times when I would have cherished having an angel with me in the room, assuring me everything would be okay.

In the months that followed I felt the same fear when I prepared to have surgery on two occasions. An angel's hand holding mine as I was wheeled into the operating room would have been treasured comfort.

But as far as I knew, I'd never seen an angel. Never. Did that mean something was wrong with me? Why did only other people have that privilege? Wasn't I spiritual enough?

Maybe you've asked the same questions. And maybe you're dissatisfied with the answers you've received. The widespread interest in angels has thrown a lot of information your way—but also confusion and contradiction and flimsy speculation. Where can you go for solid, meaningful information? How can you gain a balanced and accurate perspective that's built on God's reality and eternal truth?

That's what this book is all about.

Welcome Wonders, or a Waste of Time?

Ever since the 1990s, angels are everywhere—or rather we find them *talked about* everywhere, from major magazines and bestselling books and popular TV shows to kitchen conversations and university seminars. Lots of people say they have actually seen or felt the presence of an angel. Never in history, I suppose, has so much attention been directed at these heavenly beings as in our day.

So what's the significance of it all? Is the Lord delighted by this burst of curiosity and belief? And does he want you and me to join in the fun — or at least to take a bit more notice of angels than past generations did? Should we be looking around on earth for these heavenly beings? Should we be confident of daily care and protection from angel guardians?

Or is all this a waste of time? Maybe the angel craze that peaked in the 90s was at best just another trivial fad, and at worst a deceptive tactic of Satan's to divert people's spiritual attention away from real truth. Like young children at the Grand Canyon who can't see beyond the spoiled chipmunks darting along the rim seeking tourist handouts, if we start focusing on angels, we might miss the grand, sweeping view of God.

On the other hand, could more attention on angels actually be God's desire and plan for his people at this moment in history? Is it perhaps a clue and signal that we're on the threshold of something bigger in God's timetable for the world? Is the present age about to end? In God's mercy and love for sinners, has he caused a belief in spiritual angels to be more respectable so people can better accept the spiritual message of the gospel — before it's too late?

Or as some highly respected Bible teachers say, is there no such thing as angelic activity in our world anymore, since the close of Bible times?

The questions go on and on. (I wonder if the angels are asking them too.)

Probably no major theological issue has received as much secular attention in modern times as the doctrine of angels has in our day. You would expect Christians to be delighted at this, and start rushing in to make the most of this fresh opportunity for spiritual dialogue with the non-Christian world. But a good many Christians don't know what (if anything) to think about angels.

At least when the "God is dead" notion grabbed headlines a few decades ago, Christians were united in their response: No, they proclaimed, God is alive! But when headlines along the grocery checkout lane talk about widespread angel activity and belief in personal angels, the typical Christian reaction is: Well, maybe — or maybe not.

The Dangers

The angel craze seemed to trigger a major shift in thinking for our culture. What had once been mostly a myth to previouis generations became a fascinating reality in the popular mind. For example, more than a million people worldwide read the bimonthly Guideposts magazine *Angels on Earth*, in which each issue features a handfull of stories about people who believe they've encountered angels.

This all seems to fit into a greater openness to spirituality that's been building for years. Few people think anymore that all of life's important answers can be found in science and rational thought and reasonable logic. They know reality has another dimension — a spiritual dimension beyond science and reason. And this "other" side of reality keeps growing bigger in popular thought.

What does all this mean? Is it good or bad?

The biggest danger may well be greater susceptibility to spirituality's dark side. Mankind's mental doorway may be open wider to thinking about religion and eternity, but it's probably also open wider to Satan's influence.

Scripture warns us that "Satan himself masquerades as an angel of light" (2 Corinthians 11:14). Perhaps this strategy of deception wasn't so effective in the generations just before us. People weren't as open to believing in angels then, and if you talked about seeing one or wanting to, you might have been called flighty or foolish or weird.

Now the situation has changed. It's acceptable and even fashionable to believe in angels, and millions around the world are looking for angelic activity as never before.

But a stronger belief in angels is no guarantee of greater understanding of God's truth. The devil can ensnare us as much through "angelism" as he can through materialism or sexual lust or power-hunger. In fact he has scored some of his greatest triumphs in the disguise of angels. In the year 610 the oppressive religion of Islam was born when Muhammed received the contents of the Koran in a series of visions from someone he believed to be the angel Gabriel. Twelve centuries later, the deceptive cult of Mormonism supposedly arose when an angelic being called Moroni got Joseph Smith connected with the Book of Mormon.

Is Satan doing the same thing again? Or instead of launching a big new anti-Christian religion or cult, perhaps he and his demons are simply using angelic disguise — a little here and a little there — to flirt with people's fascinations and to create a curiosity and craving for angelic presence. By influencing the right people with the right connections to get the right books and magazine articles published and the right TV shows on the air, he can lure millions into a false sense of spiritual experience and security. The syrupy-sweet, spirit-tingling taste of a little angelism can ruin people's appetite for the good, solid food of God's Word and his gospel of grace and truth.

Even secular publications recognized at least partly this aspect of angel-mania. They noted the easy lure of preferring angels over God and describe how angels offer a form of spirituality devoid of Jesus and God. Because belief in God is no longer "popular" in America, it is possible to believe in anything. People are searching for spirituality–but not if it involves God. *Time* magazine insightfully stated, "angels are the handy compromise, all fluff and meringue, kind, nonjudgmental. They are available to everyone, like aspirin."

Life magazine attached the label "God Lite" to the angelism movement. The magazine's reporter visited a conference of angel enthusiasts. Unlike the mighty heavenly beings described in the Bible, the reporter said the angels described to him at the conference were

> a more benign and bite-size species, cuddly as a lap dog, conscientious as a school crossing guard. I heard angels likened to spiritual kissing cousins, flower delivery messengers… and just a nice feeling of warmth and love that washes all over you. Today's angels seem to spend a lot less time praising God than serving us. While they are still making super-hero, nick-of-time rescues, they are also showing up in less dire emergencies to track down a set of lost keys or make a chicken casserole more flavorful. Indeed, nearly all the angel believers I met got around to mentioning their parking space angel whom they call upon while cruising crowded city streets.

If some of your neighbors or friends or family members become attracted to an empty and frivolous but potentially dangerous angelism, will you be able to steer them out by showing them God's truth about angels? It's my prayer that this book will help you do just that. There's nothing that deals with error like a good dose of truth.

Meanwhile let's remember God is sovereign. He's shown in history that he uses even the mistakes and tragedies and follies of mankind to accomplish his higher will. Could it be that in our day he's using angelmania— even though it's often excessive and eccentric— to give his people a certain push? Does he want to sharpen our sensitivity toward spiritual realities? After all, it looks as if angels will be a big part of our eternal environment, which will be far more substantial than our short and shadowy presence on this earth. Being eternal themselves, angels have a greater claim to "reality" than our homes and jobs and hobbies. And unlike our homes and jobs and hobbies, the holy angels are always pointing us in the right direction: toward God.

Just thinking about angels can give us a fresh reminder that there's another world besides this one that clings so closely all around us. Angels already experience the fullness of that other world — God's eternal, heavenly kingdom — where God's rule goes entirely unopposed and unquestioned. Someday we'll experience it with them.

Jesus was turning our eyes toward this other, unseen world when he taught us to pray, "Thy will be done on earth as it is in heaven." Hearing those words, we easily assume that right now in heaven angels are doing God's will perfectly and gladly. So we ask the same for us, here and now. And when we sincerely pray "Thy kingdom come" to our heavenly Father, we show him that we long for something better than the enemy territory which our world is today, infested by sin and filled with deceptions from the fallen angel Satan.

The Real Thing

Before preaching and writing on this subject I read hundreds of stories describing angel sightings and encounters. Many are far-fetched and go beyond the bounds of what Scripture allows as being reliable. For example, the Bible gives no indication angels will respond if we pray directly to them for help. In fact in Scripture we don't find any instances of people even asking God to send them an angel's protection. And the only person in Scripture who tried persuading someone else to seek help from an angel was Satan, who quoted an Old Testament verse about angelic protection while tempting Jesus in the wilderness (Matthew 4:6).

More importantly, Scripture gives no basis for assuming angels will serve and help non-Christians. The Bible describes angels as "ministering spirits sent to serve *those who will inherit salvation*" (Hebrews 1:14). Who are these people destined to "inherit salvation"? The Bible makes it clear that this refers only to those who come to know Christ as Savior. It's to serve only them that angels are sent. If someone claims to have seen an angel yet that person professes no allegiance to Jesus Christ, it's likely that any angel he saw (if he truly saw one at all) was a fallen one — one of the devil's messengers, not the Lord's. Not every angel is from God.

A book far larger than the one in your hands would be needed to discuss all the circulated opinions and beliefs about angels which down through history have either been highly questionable or in flat opposition to biblical truth. But what about angel stories that fit within Bible parameters and which are reported by trustworthy sources, by people we would never expect to make things up? Should we believe them?

In his landmark 1975 book *Angels* (which has sold more than two and a half million copies and continues as a bestseller), Billy Graham collected and retold many reputable stories of experiences with angels, including this family account of his maternal grandmother's death:

> The room seemed to fill with a heavenly light. She sat up in bed and almost laughingly said, "I see Jesus. He has his arms outstretched toward me. I see Ben [her husband who had died some years earlier] and I see the angels." Then she slumped over, absent from the body but present with the Lord.

Billy Graham said he believed in angels not only because of the Bible's testimony about them, but also "because I have sensed their presence in my life on special occasions." He wrote:

> As an evangelist, I have often felt too far spent to minister from the pulpit to men and women who have filled stadiums to hear a message from the Lord. Yet again and again my weakness has vanished, and my strength has been renewed. I have been filled with God's power not only in my soul but physically. On many occasions, God has become especially real, and has sent his unseen angelic visitors to touch my body and let me be his messenger for heaven, speaking as a dying man to dying men.

He also recounted such exciting stories as this one from pioneer missionary John G. Paton in the New Hebrides Islands, in the South Pacific:

Hostile natives surrounded his mission headquarters one night, intent on burning the Patons out and killing them. John Paton and his wife prayed all during that terror-filled night that God would deliver them. When daylight came they were amazed to see that, unaccountably, the attackers had left. They thanked God for delivering them.

A year later, the chief of the tribe was converted to Jesus Christ, and Mr. Paton, remembering what had happened, asked the chief what had kept him and his men from burning down the house and killing them. The chief replied in surprise, "Who were all those men you had with you there?" The missionary answered, "There were no men there; just my wife and I." The chief argued that they had seen many men standing guard — hundreds of big men in shining garments with drawn swords in their hands. They seemed to circle the mission station so that the natives were afraid to attack. Only then did Mr. Paton realize that God had sent his angels to protect them. The chief agreed that there was no other explanation.

One of the most popular angel stories of this century happened in a gruesome Nazi prison camp in the Second World War, as told by Corrie ten Boom in *A Prisoner — And Yet.* She and her sister Betsie had just arrived at Ravensbruck, where new prisoners were being searched. Corrie was hiding a Bible under her dress.

It did bulge out obviously through my dress; but I prayed, "Lord, cause now Thine angels to surround me; and let them not be transparent today, for the guards must not see me." I felt perfectly at ease. Calmly I passed the guards. Everyone was checked, from the front, the sides, the back. Not a bulge escaped the eyes of the guard. The woman just in front of me had hidden a woolen vest under her dress; it was taken from her. They let me pass, for they did not see me. Betsie, right behind me, was searched.

But outside awaited another danger. On each side of the door were women who looked everyone over for a second time. They felt over the body of each one who passed. I knew they would not see me, for the angels were still surrounding me. I was not even surprised when they passed me by; but within me rose the jubilant cry, "O Lord, if Thou dost so answer prayer, I can face even Ravensbruck unafraid."

Christianity Today reported a story of angelic intervention told by the editor of *Leadership*, a magazine for church leaders. One night the editor's young daughter was in a coma and near death. A hospital staff worker looked into the girl's room and witnessed an astonishing sight: Angels were hovering over the girl's bed.

Amazingly, the following morning the daughter had recovered. Her father, a man not prone to sensationalism, did not hesitate to believe angels had truly visited his daughter. Meanwhile the hospital worker renewed her commitment to God as a result of what she had seen in the girl's room that night.

A Reliable Source

Stories like these are from sources we've come to trust. So do people really see angels today? If so, who are these angels, and what in the world are they doing?

We'll look at these and many other questions in this book. And the Bible will be our guide. Actually there's nowhere else reliable to look. We would know nothing dependable about angels if it weren't for the fact that God himself has told us. Apart from divine revelation, science and human wisdom can't come close to answering our questions on this topic, and would only mumble and stumble along through speculation. The Bible, however, as Lewis Sperry Chafer reminds us, reflects God's knowledge of the universe rather than man's; therefore in the Scriptures the angels, concerning whom man of himself could know nothing, are introduced with perfect freedom.

Scripture is our source and standard. Much that goes on in the name of angels in our world isn't biblical; we need caution not to get caught in the web of angelmania. Whatever our past experiences or beliefs or opinions regarding angels, they must be checked against the principles of Scripture. They must spring from Scripture, not from what we've conjured up in our minds that we'd *like* to believe about angels.

Don't worry that limiting our authority to God's Word will make this a dull subject. In that "perfect freedom" of disclosure that Chafer noted, what the Bible says about angels is stirring and eye-opening and heart-opening.

Therefore we can enter gladly and easily into an experience with angels any time we like. God has given us rich and inspired messages in Scripture that usher us right into the essence of what angels are all about. God's Book is the thrilling place and the trustworthy place to learn about them. We can see them and hear them and watch them work, and find out all that their examples can teach us. Through careful study, anyone who truly seeks the Lord with a good and honest heart can find these riches.

And yet for all that the Scriptures tell us about angels, the serious Bible student soon gets the feeling God has been guarded in what he's revealed. Everything Scripture says concerning angels is in connection to something else as the main theme. There are no pages or passages whose central purpose is to spell out a doctrine of angels. So we can't uncover as much about them as we might like. Unfortunately those who don't understand or appreciate the Bible's wisdom and authority have been quick to jump in and try to fill all the gaps with fanciful conjecture. We ought to try to know as much about angels as God has determined to reveal to us — and then be content to leave it at that. Someday we'll understand more. But try crossing that line now and you can end up doing yourself damage.

It's like our knowledge of heaven. We really don't know much about it. The bottom line is that heaven is where God is, which is all that should be important. The writer of Psalm 73 shows the right heart when he tells God, "Whom have I in heaven but you? And earth has nothing I desire besides you." Besides God there is no one on earth and no one in heaven — not even angels — who can give your soul true fulfillment.

So make sure God sets your agenda, whatever knowledge you seek. John Calvin worded it this way as he launched his own discussion of angels:

> Let us here remember that on the whole subject of religion one rule of modesty and soberness is to be observed, and it is this — in obscure matters not to speak or think, or even long to know, more than the Word of God has delivered.

So what does the Word of God deliver to us about angels? How much does God really want us to comprehend about this mysterious subject?

Let's explore the answers together.

Angels and Me and You

But first come back with me to that fall day, when I found out I had cancer. I never did see or hear an angel in the room with me, as much as that might have encouraged me then. But I did feel God's presence. And who's to say seeing an angel would have been better than that?

Both times that I went into surgery, I found a peace in my heart that was born out of my relationship with God. Looking back on those months I wonder what an angel could have added to that peace — except perhaps another exclamation point to my belief that God was there, caring for me.

So as I think about why some people see angels and others don't, I wonder if God doesn't withhold the sight of angels from most of us so we'll understand where our trust should truly be and where we really should focus our attention. Maybe we don't need all the sensations and excitement that so many people clamor for. Wonderful as the presence of an angel might be, God has given us something better. In fact he's given us the greatest gift of all: his presence through his Holy Spirit, and in his Word.

Maybe it's even possible that the lack of an angelic manifestation in my life is like a backhanded compliment. God may be telling me, "Jeremiah, you don't need an angel. You'll be fine. You know who you are and Who is with you—and that's enough for now."

If an angel has never made himself known to you either, maybe you can take it as God's affirmation of your trust in him. And if someday in the future God deems it wise and good to dispatch an angel to me or to you, I'm sure he will. I don't have a fixation on angels, but I'm more convinced than ever that they are far more involved in our world than most of us realize. I believe they certainly do intervene here, both visibly and invisibly.

Meanwhile, whether or not we ever see an angel before we're carried home to heaven, there's great value in exploring what God has to say about them. As C. F. Dickason reminds us in his biblical handbook *Angels: Elect and Evil,*

> Though angelology is not a cardinal doctrine, its acceptance opens the mind to a better understanding of the Bible, God's plan of the ages, the Christian life and ministry, as well as world conditions and the course of world affairs.

If studying this subject has anything close to the impact on you that it already has had on me, your mind and heart will soon be opened to believe a host of things you may never before have realized. There's a lot more to this "strange" topic of angels than we imagine. Once we honestly investigate the amazing things Scripture tells us about them, we actually find ourselves drawn closer to God, instead of being distracted and turned away from him. Anyone who goes into a study of angels with a high view of God will come away with an even higher view.

That, in fact, is the only sufficient aim in a study of angels: that you might draw closer to God. If you study angels and the result is anything less —if you build up only a file of information about angels or a fascination with them or even a supposed relationship with one, but haven't encountered at least a tug toward humble submission to the Almighty God…you've totally missed what angels are all about.

Chapter Two

IN THE PRESENCE
OF ANGELS—Part I

D O YOU *really* believe in angels?

Walt Shepard does. His angel story is a favorite among hundreds I've read.

Walt had become depressed over a broken relationship and was ready to end his life. In the dark, predawn hours one Sunday he accelerated his Sunbeam sports car to 120 miles per hour on Interstate 10, north of New Orleans.

Ahead, on the side of the road, he saw what appeared to be an abandoned car. Here was his chance, he decided.

He plowed into the back of the parked car. There was an explosion. Both vehicles burst into flames.

The manager of a nearby motel heard the crash and called rescue authorities.

Walt had been thrown through his windshield and was lying on the mangled engine, trapped by the crumpled hood. Fire surrounded him. He lost consciousness.

The highway patrol quickly arrived but the fire was so intense it kept officers from getting within fifty feet of the wreckage. With amazement, however, they and the hotel manager suddenly saw two figures approach the car without hesitation. They pulled Walt from the flames, then helped a rescue team load him in an ambulance. The ambulance sped away.

The officers wanted to interview the two unknown helpers to find out more about the accident and to write up reckless driving charges against Walt. Though no other cars had been parked nearby, the two had mysteriously disappeared.

Walt began months of painful recovery. He struggled with bitterness and anger. But he began reflecting on his upbringing as the son of Presbyterian missionaries.

One day he decided to pray. He was in a body cast and couldn't kneel, but he rolled over in his bed and faced the wall. He said to the Lord, "I can't take it. I need your forgiveness…. Come into my life and clean me up."

The next morning he woke up after the best night's rest he could remember in five years.

His father, meanwhile, had talked with those who witnessed his son's rescue. They agreed that two unidentified figures had boldly approached the car as though there were no fire at all. The rescue continued to baffle police.

A short time after Walt prayed his prayer, he was talking with his dad about the unusual circumstances of the accident. His father proposed a supernatural explanation.

"Son, I think you were saved by two angels," he said, "so you'd have the opportunity to do what you did this week — to get your life right with God."

At first Walt was skeptical. But now, after maturing from youth to middle age, he says, "I believe angels are simply part of God's natural dealings with us. It's amazing, but I believe angels rescued me from the fire that morning. And I believe they haven't stopped working."

Do you believe Walt Shepard's story? I can't verify it, but in my opinion his account fits the context of everything the Bible tells us angels can do and will do. Walt's story is strong because it has the right focus. It gives glory to God — as angels do — and credits God with using angels to help bring salvation through Jesus Christ to a man's soul.

A Settled Question

Some people might criticize you believing in angels or even expressing interest in them. Maybe you've already heard from critics like that. But don't let them worry you. You're in better company than they are.

In the Scriptures—from Genesis to Revelation—the existence of angels is simply assumed. The Bible contains more than three hundred direct references to them.

The same assumption about the reality of angels has always been widespread throughout our civilization. "There is nothing unnatural or contrary to reason" about a belief in angels, wrote J. M. Wilson earlier in this century. "Indeed the warm welcome human nature has always given to this thought is an argument in its favor. Why should there not be such an order of beings...?" In 1952 the editorial board of the classic series *Great Books of the Western World* included "Angels" as one of the 102 most important topics and ideas that the famous authors of these great books have discussed down through the ages. Throughout the full length of history, skepticism about angels has been the minority view, though it began to swell when faith in science replaced faith in God.

Those who have doubts might run the risk of suffering the same fate as the Sadducees, the only group of folks identified in the Bible as not believing in angels (Acts 23:8). Such "gross ignorance," as John Calvin called it, was a point that put even the hypocritical Pharisees ahead of them. The Sadducees disappeared from history without a trace before the first century ended, though in Jesus' day they were Israel's most powerful Jews. They controlled both the high priesthood and the Sanhedrin, the Jewish ruling council. They were aristocratic, pragmatic, and arrogant — quite a contrast to the childlike faith that so easily believes in angels.

It's richly satisfying to see in Acts 5 how God chose to thwart the Sadducees in their actions against his apostles. After seeing the apostles heal the sick and powerfully proclaim the gospel, we read in Acts 5:17-18 that "the high priest and all his associates, who were members of the party of the Sadducees, were filled with jealousy. They arrested the apostles and put them in the public jail."

Now God's chosen method for correcting this injustice is unveiled in verses 19-21:

> But during the night *an angel of the Lord* opened the doors of the jail and brought them out. "Go, stand in the temple courts," he said, "and tell the people the full message of this new life." At daybreak they entered the temple courts, as they had been told, and began to teach the people.

The apostles might have held back a few laughs shortly after this episode when they were summoned once more before that no-such-thing-as-angels crowd. The powerful Sadducees spurned angels, and would drop from history within a generation; the imprisoned apostles simply obeyed God's message delivered by an angel, and they would change history's course forever.

An equally ironic but more poignant picture of the hardened Sadducees comes later in Acts, when Stephen was dragged before the Sadducee-dominated Sanhedrin. Stephen, "a man full of God's grace and power" (6:8), had been falsely accused of blasphemy. At his trial, "all who were sitting in the Sanhedrin looked intently at Stephen, and they saw that his face was like the face of an *angel*" (6:15). But angelic appearance wasn't enough to prevent the blinded Sadducees from stoning Stephen to death.

One last word before dropping for good the fundamental but easily answered question of whether angels exist. J. M. Wilson states it well:

> For the Christian the whole question turns on the weight to be attached to the words of our Lord. All are agreed that he teaches the existence, reality, and activity of angelic beings.... We have the guarantee of Christ's word for the existence of angels; for most Christians that will settle the question.

IN THE PRESENCE OF ANGELS—Part I   31

Yes. For you and me and our brothers and sisters who follow Christ —
as we acknowledge the lordship of Jesus and the "guarantee of Christ's word"
— the question is settled already. For the rest, doubts will surely evaporate
on the day "when the Son of Man comes in his glory, *and all the angels with
him*" (Matthew 25:31).

No Other Choice

Okay, our critics may respond, so angels exist. But why should that interest
us?

There are some, for example, who suppose there's no angelic activity on
earth today since we live in the time of the Holy Spirit. However, a quick
look at Acts 8 should answer their objection. Notice who helps and guides
Philip into a life-saving mission. First we read, "Now *an angel of the Lord* said
to Philip, 'Go south to the road — the desert road — that goes down from
Jerusalem to Gaza.' So he started out...." (8:26-27).

Down that desert road Philip spotted someone riding in a chariot and
reading a book. Philip was now ready for further guidance from God.
Would the angel reappear? No. Now we read, "*The Spirit* told Philip, 'Go to
that chariot and stay near it.' Then Philip ran up to the chariot..." (8:29-30).

Here we see the Holy Spirit and an angel working together, and Philip
responding correctly, just as the jailed apostles had done earlier. The result
for Philip was the privilege of leading the chariot-rider — a visiting dignitary
from Ethiopia — to salvation.

Perhaps the Spirit himself directed the angel on that occasion. We know
God the Father commands angels, and we also see in Scripture that his Son
Jesus can. While facing arrest, Jesus claimed he could just say the word and
his Father would "at once put *at my disposal* more than twelve legions of
angels" (Matthew 26:53). Before Jesus ascended he told his disciples, "All
authority *in heaven* and on earth has been given to me" (28:18) — certainly
his authority in heaven includes authority over angels.

So if God can direct angels and Jesus can direct angels, it's easy to believe that the third Person of the Trinity can as well. The Holy Spirit is eternal God, not just a modern-day substitute for angels. And I see no clear indication in Scripture whatsoever that angelic activity will decline or cease in this day, the age in which Jesus Christ is building his church through the Holy Spirit's power.

Meanwhile other critics accept the possibility of modern angelic activity but don't think the topic is worth close study. Sure, angels are out there somewhere, these people say, and we can all be pleasantly impressed with them when we get to heaven and actually see them. But why bother *now* to scrutinize what the Bible says about them?

Why? Because ultimately God leaves us no other option. As theologian M. J. Erickson declares,

> The teaching of Scripture is that he has created these spiritual beings and has chosen to carry out many of his acts through them. Therefore, if we are to be faithful students of the Bible, we have no choice but to speak of these beings.

We run the risk of insulting God if we aren't truly open to appreciate every single thing he's made — including angels — as well as to *learn* about God from everything he's made — including angels, and perhaps *especially* angels. "If we desire to know God by his works," wrote Calvin, "we surely cannot overlook this noble and illustrious specimen."

The great hymn from Stuart K. Hines captures the right mindset:

> O Lord my God, when I in awesome wonder
> Consider *all* the works Thy hands have made...
> Then sings my soul, my Savior God, to Thee:
> How great Thou art, how great Thou art!

"Awesome wonder" is the perfect phrase to describe a person's frame of mind after a true biblical exploration of angels.

But enough of the awesome wonder talk, some would say. What about *pragmatic* value?

This is probably the most deeply founded objection to studying about angels. Always faithful to watch out for number one, our down-to-earth spirit demands: What's in it for me?

Well — quite a lot, as we'll see. A. C. Gaebelein's conviction in *The Angels of God* points the way:

> Like every truth, the truth of the angels of God — their presence on earth and their loving ministries — has a practical value. As we realize in faith … that they are watching us, ready to walk with us as we walk with him in his ways, ready to serve us as we serve him, ready to shield us and help us in a hundred different ways, a solemn feeling will come into our lives. Surely we will walk softly in the presence of the Lord and his holy angels…. Thus this truth will assist us in a holy life.

Finally, there's another big point to make about the *why* of studying angels before we continue on to taste the riches. It's a point that's truer today than it was yesterday, and will be truer tomorrow than it is today.

Most Christians agree demonic activity will increase as we near the last days. It's a viewpoint grounded not only in simple observation of what the world is coming to, but also in Scripture. "The Spirit clearly says," Paul reminds us in 1 Timothy 4:1, "that in later times some will abandon the faith and follow deceiving spirits and things taught by demons."

Here in our own church's counseling ministry we've seen this a lot. After reviewing some of the powerful and mystifying disorders people are manifesting, we look at each other and say, "Something's going on here that isn't human." It's true for Christian ministry throughout the world too: We have seen and will probably continue to see greater attacks from the forces of spiritual evil.

So I ask you: Isn't it reasonable to expect that as demonic activity increases while we near the day of the Lord's return, angelic activity will also increase? It makes sense. As Billy Graham says, "God is still in business too."

Warriors and Agents of Wrath

So hold on to your book and let's go for a ride—a journey at the speed of heavenly light across the ages and pages of Scripture.

We have a guide going with us, both to pilot our invisible craft and to explain things along the way. He's a stranger, but he seems a nice enough fellow. In a cheerful voice he tells us we'll be watching the angels at work. "Put everything else out of mind," he says. "Use all your mental powers to catch the clearest impression of what angels do and how they do it. We'll take several spins through the territory, and each time our perspective will change a little, so there's something new to learn at each turn." It sounds like an interesting trip.

"Ready?" he says. We nod.

"Let's go!"

Our first stop is at the eastern gateway to the Garden of Eden. Our guide tells us this is the first glimpse in Scripture of angelic creatures. It's by no means a peaceful, pleasant scene. What catches our attention first is a flaming sword flashing back and forth. These heavenly beings are armed soldiers placed here by the Holy God because his holy creation has just been contaminated by the sin of Adam and Eve. The soldiers' mission: "to guard the way to the tree of life." We can tell they mean business. We have no intention of even a peek over their shoulders at the tree. (*Genesis 3:24*)

Now we zoom forward across the centuries. We look down on a small city crowning a hill. This is Jerusalem, city of David. Between the town's largest buildings we see a figure kneeling in the street, looking up at the sky. Yes, our guide tells us, that's David himself.

Our eyes blink, catching a movement in the clouds above. We turn to look where David looks. We gasp, overcome by what we sense and see, something words can't fully describe: The angel of the Lord is there. At once we're given insight to know the situation. In the angel's hand is a sword holding the power of the plague. Throughout the land of Israel this day, sickness from that sword has already killed seventy thousand people.

Now the angel stretches his hand over Jerusalem. The sword is poised to strike.

In the street below, a voice cries out. David confesses in agony: "I am the one who sinned!"

Another voice shouts like thunder, far above the angel: "Enough! Withdraw your hand." The angel puts the sword back in its sheath. (2 Samuel 24:15-17, 1 Chronicles 21:14-17)

We move forward again through time to a different scene. Now we see more soldiers—human soldiers—massed as an army, countless thousands upon thousands. Outside the gates of Jerusalem their camp stretches as far as we can see in the evening light. These are Assyrians, living legends for their battle-skill and their cruelty as conquerors.

Night comes on. In time the campfires and the boasting voices die down. The vast camp grows quiet. The soldiers sleep, resting for tomorrow's work of war against the besieged city.

The darkness deepens. Suddenly we look up and cringe. There he is again—the angel of the Lord, come to slay.

His deed is done in only a moment. Then the angel is gone.

We watch. The camp is cloaked in quietness as before, only more so. Dawn's first grayness marks a faint line in the sky behind the city. Still the camp does not awaken. The light grows, revealing nothing in the sprawling Assyrian camp except dead bodies. Their number is more than would later be killed at Hiroshima and Nagasaki combined. In a single night, an angel has slain one hundred eighty-five thousand Assyrians. (2 Kings 19:35, 2 Chronicles 32:21, Isaiah 37:36)

Forward again, seven hundred years. We see another king over Israel. He wears rich robes and is seated on a throne while addressing an admiring throng. The people shout: "This is the voice of a god and not a man! Long live the god King Herod!"

Herod's plump face glows. He extends his open, meaty palms to acknowledge the acclaim. He does not see what we see: An angel of the Lord suddenly stands behind the throne, and touches the king's body. Herod's smile slackens. He bends over in pain. He feels but does not know what is happening: Worms are devouring him from within. (*Acts 12:21-23*)

Forward, forward again we go, to view a raging battlefield. The time and scene are hazy — we're beyond earth and outside earthly time. The fiery, deafening intensity of the fight is beyond anything we've imagined or could ever explain. In fact we can bear only a moment of it before the image disappears. But we remember what we saw: "There was war in heaven. Michael and his angels fought against the dragon, and the dragon and his angels fought back." (*Revelation 12:7*)

The next scenes in our journey come as fleeting glimpses into the future. They flare into our view for only a second or so. After the last picture has dissolved, we struggle to express in words what we saw and perceived.

First, four angels stood on a riverbank and "were released to kill a third of mankind."

Then seven angels appeared and were given "seven golden bowls filled with the wrath of God."

Seven more scenes followed immediately. In each brief picture, one of the seven angels poured out his bowl upon a world in rebellion against God. Instantly, calamity struck. We trembled as we saw the unleashed angelic power: "Ugly and painful sores broke out on the people." "Every living thing in the sea died." "The rivers and springs of water...became blood." "The sun was given power to scorch people with fire." There was darkness. There was drought. There was an earthquake more powerful than any in history, and a storm of hundred-pound hailstones. (*Revelation 9:14-15, 15:1, 15:6, 16:1-21*)

And now another scene. This one lingers in view for a longer while. We look up. Out of a golden brightness that we know is heaven, an angel rapidly descends. In one hand he holds a huge key. In the other is a massive chain. He carries the chain effortlessly enough, but it looks as if it must weigh tons.

Now we see where the angel goes. Below, a serpentine dragon lashes about, breathing fire and fury. If it weren't for the presence of the descending angel we would scream in horror, for the dragon is Satan, revealed in all his raw and ugly power.

The angel nears. With only one hand he casts out a short length of the chain and snares the dragon at once. Satan is paralyzed, powerless before him. Still using only one hand, the angel wraps the chain around and around and around the dragon. The mighty chain seems endless; not until the angel makes exactly a thousand loops does the last link lock in place.

Now the angel touches the key to the ground. The surface cracks wide and a gaping hole opens. With his free hand the angel picks up the bound dragon and tosses him into the bottomless blackness. (*Revelation 20:1-3*)

In silence, this final picture fades. Our guide tells us that the first leg of our journey is over. Soberly we tell each other that all this has done something to our view of angels. Divorced from any credibility forever in our minds are the thoughts of plump baby "cherubs" or pale ladies with see-through wings traced in glitter across our Christmas cards.

No, real angels have been and are and shall forever be awesome *warriors* for God, agents of his wrath and power. We don't wonder in the least why people in the Bible who see angels are so often struck with terror at the sight.

And we look forward to what we'll discover on the next stretch of our journey.

Chapter Three

IN THE PRESENCE
OF ANGELS—Part II

O
UR HEARTS are still thumping, but our guide says it's time to move again.

We race to another scene from centuries past. Not far away we see a walled city dotted with palm trees—Jericho. At a distance outside the city, a man crouches behind rocks and bushes. He keeps himself hidden from the watchmen on the walls as he moves in closer. This is Joshua, scouting out the scene for the battle he expects shortly between Jericho's defenders and the army of Israel camped nearby.

But he's not alone. Another warrior arrived here first. As Joshua parts some branches to pass through a clump of shrubbery, he sees the man, and stops cold. It's too late to slip back undetected. The warrior is looking right at him, with drawn sword in his hand.

Bravely Joshua moves closer. He plants his feet only five paces from the warrior. Joshua's hand rests on his sword hilt. Somehow he is sure this man knows his identity. But Joshua is filled with a strange uncertainty about the man.

Joshua gets to the point: "Are you for us, or for our enemies?"

"Neither," the warrior answers. "But I have come as the commander of the army of the Lord." Joshua knows at once what he means. This is the captain of the Lord's angelic host, the holy army whose service transcends any earthly allegiance, even to Israel. A rush of fear mixed with hope surges through him. Will God's angels fight for Israel against Jericho?

Joshua throws himself down. With his face bowed to the ground he asks for a message from the Lord.

"Take off your sandals," the commander says, "for this place is holy." Joshua removes his sandals.

"Jericho is delivered into your hands," the commander continues. Then he outlines step by step what Joshua and the armies of Israel must do to bring to pass the victory God has already ordained. *(Joshua 5:13–6:5)*

Onward again. Centuries later we're in rugged forest country in the south of Judah. Nearly hidden on a hillside is a cave. At its mouth, and as far inside as the late afternoon light will reveal, we can see a few men — they are from David's band. A few of them stand watch, but most are resting from their latest flight from the soldiers of King Saul. They are weary but thankful to be safe.

From the depths of the cave David himself walks out. The few men outside greet him and slap his shoulders. David laughs with them, then saunters down the hill away through the trees to a place where he can be alone. He carries a simple harp. By a small stream at the foot of the hill he sits down. He's silent for a long time as he looks from the trickling water to the wind-tossed trees and up to the clouds. Sometimes he bows his head and closes his eyes. We sense a divine presence around this man. In quiet respect we hardly dare to breathe as we watch.

Finally David takes up his harp and his fingers pluck forth a melody. In his strong, pleasing voice he begins a new song. He sings praise and thanksgiving. And he sings his faith in God's protection:

> *The angel of the Lord*
> *encamps around those who fear him,*
> *and he delivers them.*

With a smile David looks to either side, trusting in the angel's invisible presence. Then he sings his new song again. (Psalm 34:7)

Forward now five hundred years and five hundred miles. We're in Babylon, where the Jewish people have been taken captive. King Nebuchadnezzar is seated on a portable throne set up near a towering furnace —a furnace built for executions. At the bottom of the furnace-tower is a door, and cut into it is a window of thick Phoenician glass. The throne is positioned so the king can look through the glass and watch the flames torture the offenders whom he has judged.

Suddenly the king leaps to his feet, his arm outstretched, his hand pointing. Three Jews who refused to bow down and worship Nebuchadnezzar had been dropped into the flames from the top of the tower. Yet now the king sees not three figures but four. All stand calm amid the flames, unharmed. And the fourth figure is surrounded by a whiteness that shines even brighter than the flames. He looks like a being from heaven! And his arms reach out to enfold the others.

The king orders the furnace door opened. He shouts inside: "Shadrach, Meshach, and Abednego, servants of the Most High God, come out!" They do. As soon as the third man emerges, the fourth figure inside disappears.

Shadrach, Meshach, and Abednego stride forward and stand before the king's throne. The ropes with which they were tied have burnt off, but nothing else about them has even the smell of smoke.

Nebuchadnezzar takes a step toward them, then drops to his knees and cries, "Praise be to the God of Shadrach, Meshach, and Abednego, who has sent his angel to rescue his servants!" (Daniel 3:13-30)

We go forward to another day under another king in Babylon. In the first light of dawn, King Darius rushes to the great stone-and-iron enclosure where Babylon's lions are kept. He orders the servant with him to pull back the stone that was rolled over the opening to the den. Before the stone is halfway back Darius rushes forward and grips the iron bars on the grated gate. "Daniel," he cries, "your God whom you always worship—has he been able to rescue you from the lions?"

From the darkness in the den comes a man's calm and confident voice with a greeting for the king. And he adds, "Yes, my God sent his angel, and he shut the mouth of the lions." (Daniel 6:19-22)

Forward again to see another gate with iron bars, the door to a cell in a Jerusalem prison. In the flickering light of a nearby torch we see the apostle Peter asleep between two soldiers. Each of his arms is bound by a separate chain. Suddenly the cell fills with light. An angel of the Lord stands there, but neither Peter nor the soldiers stir from their sleep. The angel reaches out and delivers a good whack to Peter's side. The chains fall from Peter's wrists and drop noisily to the floor. Peter's eyes slowly open, but we're amazed to see the guards still sleeping.

"Get up!" the angel loudly commands Peter. "And get dressed." Peter obeys and silently follows the angel out of the cell and past two sets of guards, but he still seems half asleep. The last iron gate separating the prison from the city streets opens by itself. Peter and the angel walk through. The cool night air is bracing. Peter's eyes open wider.

Without a word they walk side by side to the end of the street. Peter turns to look down a side street leading to the house where he last saw his friends and fellow disciples—before he was hauled off to jail.

He turns back around. He's alone. His companion is gone.

In the deserted street, under stars shining in the blackness, Peter speaks aloud: "The Lord sent his angel to rescue me." (Acts 12:11)

The second part of our journey is finished, our guide announces. We've been inspired and encouraged to see how God sends his angels to *deliver* and *protect* and *defend* his people. We smile and say that already we expect to sleep more soundly tonight.

"But first," says our guide, "there's still much more to see as well as to hear. In fact, on this next leg of the journey, your ears will be of more value than your eyes."

Guidance from God

He's taking us faster now. We're on a desert road near a spring where a woman kneels to drink from the water. Suddenly we see an angel approaching on the road.

"Hagar, servant of Sarai," he calls. "Where have you come from and where are you going?"

Hagar looks up. "I'm running away from my mistress Sarai," she answers.

"Go back to your mistress," the angel commands, "and submit to her." (Genesis 16:7-9)

The scene changes to an early morning on the plain west of the Dead Sea. Two angels rush out the city gate of Sodom. They're holding the hands of Lot and his wife and his daughters, pulling them along. At a good distance from the gate they finally halt and let go of the hands of Lot and his family. "Now flee for your lives!" one of the angels commands. "Don't look back and don't stop anywhere in the plain! Flee to the mountains or you'll be swept away!" (Genesis 19:15-17)

Next we see the shepherd Jacob asleep in the land of the eastern peoples, where he works for his father-in-law. We can see into Jacob's dream. God's angel speaks to him: "Leave this land at once and go back to your native land." (Genesis 31:10-13)

Now we're startled by thunder and lightning and smoke. We're on Mount Sinai with Moses. God calls to him from the thunder. "See, I am sending an angel ahead of you to guard you along the way and to bring you to the place I have prepared. Pay attention to him and listen to what he says." (Exodus 23:20-21)

Next we're on a path between two walled vineyards. The angel of the Lord stands with drawn sword. The man Balaam bows to the ground before the angel. Balaam's donkey, with a satisfied look on his gray, gnarly face, is nearby. The angel says to Balaam, "Go, but speak only what I tell you." (Numbers 22:22-35)

We're on a hilltop now along the ridge of Mount Carmel. Dressed in a hairy garb tied with a leather belt, the prophet Elijah waits. A captain with fifty soldiers approaches in the valley below, sent by the wicked King Ahab. This is the third of Ahab's captains and the third set of fifty men to come up this valley on the same mission. Both times before, they demanded Elijah's surrender to Ahab. Each time, Elijah called down fire from heaven to destroy them all.

The third captain is more humble. He falls on his knees and calls up to the prophet, "Please have respect for my life and the lives of these fifty men!"

Immediately the angel of the Lord comes to Elijah's side and speaks: "Go down with him; do not be afraid of him." Elijah gathers his cloak and steps down the hillside to go with Ahab's captain. (2 Kings 1)

Now we're in Jerusalem once more, in the time of the plague that struck the entire land during David's reign. We're in the house of an older man who kneels in prayer. He's a prophet named Gad. He's a longtime friend of the king's, and first helped him many years ago when the young David was fleeing from Saul.

As Gad prays, the angel of the Lord comes to him with clear instructions: "Tell David to go up and build an altar to the Lord on the threshing floor of Araunah the Jebusite." The angel leaves, and the prophet goes to find his king. (1 Chronicles 21:18)

Next we're in a small and simple house in the town of Nazareth in Galilee, at night. A worried young man tosses in restless sleep. In his dream an angel of the Lord appears and says, "Joseph son of David, don't be afraid to bring Mary home as your wife. The child conceived in her is from the Holy Spirit." (Matthew 1:20)

Later we see the same man resting deeply and peacefully in a house in Bethlehem. Again in his dream he sees and hears the angel: "Get up! Take the child and his mother and escape to Egypt. Stay there until I tell you, for Herod will look for the child to kill him." Joseph opens his eyes. He's on his feet at once. (Matthew 2:13)

Forward now to another house, larger and better furnished. We're in the Mediterranean port of Caesarea, headquarters of a Roman regiment occupying Palestine. A man wearing a centurion's uniform is kneeling in prayer.

Suddenly an angel in shining clothes is standing in the room behind him. "Cornelius!" he calls.

The centurion turns and stares in fear. "What is it, Lord?"

"Your prayers and gifts to the poor have come up as a memorial offering before God," the angel replies. "Now send men to Joppa to bring back a man named Simon Peter. He's a guest in the home of Simon the tanner, who lives by the sea."

The angel departs. With quick, military-like obedience to the angel's words, Cornelius calls in two servants. He also calls one of his aides who, like Cornelius, believes in God. Cornelius tells them everything the angel said and sends the three on their way to Joppa. (*Acts 10:3-23*)

More thunder now. We're back in the future, where the apostle John is in the middle of a blinding revelation. He sees an angel "robed in a cloud, with a rainbow above his head; his face was like the sun." The angel has his right foot planted on the sea; his left is on the land. He holds a scroll, looking so small in his massive hand.

John hears a voice from heaven: "Go, take the scroll that lies open in the hand of the angel who is standing on the sea and on the land." Somehow John is empowered to move and to reach into the cloud-robed angel's hand. The angel looks down to him and says, "Take it and eat it. It will turn your stomach sour, but in your mouth it will be as sweet as honey." (*Revelation 10:1-10*)

Another portion of our journey has ended. "What have you learned from your listening?" the guide asks.

We answer, "That angels give *guidance* from God, with clear and specific instructions."

Our guide nods. Then he starts us out again.

Comfort and Encouragement

We're going even faster now. "This time watch the angels' hands," the guide says.

We're back in the desert again, with the woman we saw earlier at the spring. This time no water is in sight. The woman is seated in the hot sand, her face buried in her hands, her shoulders heaving. A few steps away under the meager shade of a scrub bush, a boy cries with a parched, rasping voice.

Suddenly, high above us in a stark blue sky, an angel appears. He calls down, "What is the matter, Hagar? Don't be afraid. God has heard the boy crying as he lies there. Lift the boy up and take him by the hand." Hagar rises. Clutching her own dry throat, she shuffles in a daze through the sand to her crying son.

Above her the angel sweeps his hand over the scene. Hagar turns. She sees for the first time what we hadn't noticed before either: a well of water close by. (*Genesis 21:14-19*)

Now we move on to another desert scene where we see Elijah again. He hurries with stumbling steps, as if he's run a long way. Finally, in the shade of a broom bush, he falls to the ground. Gasping, he prays: "I've had enough, Lord. Please take my life!" He collapses into an exhausted sleep.

All at once an angel is bending over Elijah, touching his shoulder. "Get up," the angel says, "and eat."

Elijah weakly lifts himself from the ground. He's as surprised as we are at what the angel points to: a fire of hot coals, with a pan of bread baking over it. A toasty brown crust and a delicious aroma tell us that it's ready to eat. A pottery jar of water is nearby, cool enough to be covered with beads of moisture.

"Eat and drink," the angel tells Elijah, "for your journey ahead is too much for you." (1 Kings 19:3-7)

Once more we're with Daniel in Babylon. He's become an old man, though still strong. He and a few companions stroll along a bank of the great Tigris River. Suddenly there's a roar and a blaze of light. His companions flee in terror, but Daniel stays to see a blinding, thundering vision of a heavenly being. As he gazes, he feels his strength draining. He falls, fully outstretched on the ground along the riverbank.

The angel touches Daniel and helps him to his hands and knees. "Daniel," he says, "you're a man highly esteemed. Stand up and consider carefully the words I will speak to you." Somehow Daniel stands.

The angel tells him not to be afraid. He says he's come in response to Daniel's prayers, though he had to overcome demonic opposition on the way. "Now I'm here," the angel adds, "to tell you what will happen to your people in the future."

Once more Daniel swoons and falls to his knees. His head lowers to the ground. He wants to talk, but words will not come. Again he is helped by an angel's touch — this time to his lips. Daniel opens his mouth. In halting words he explains the anguish and weakness he feels. "My strength is gone," he whispers. "I can hardly breathe."

The angel touches him again and says, "Do not be afraid, O man highly esteemed. Peace! Be strong now. Be strong!"

Soon Daniel's shoulders pull back, his chin lifts, and his chest begins to rise and fall in the rhythm of regular breathing. "Speak now, my lord," he tells the angel, "since you've given me strength." (Daniel 10:4-19)

Again we're in the desert, in a specially rocky and barren tract. For the first time on this journey we see Jesus Christ, Son of Man and Son of God. He stands on a shadeless, stony hill.

Over the horizon a shadowy form is departing. Satan was here, tempting Jesus, but for now he's gone.

Our Master's body and face are thin from forty days of fasting. His skin is darkened by the sun.

Now, coming in visible form — just as the devil came — a group of angels appear at the side of Jesus. They kneel before him and reach out to him with food. (*Matthew 4:10-11; Mark 1:13*)

Forward now, but we're still with Jesus. It is night, and we're in an olive grove. A stone's throw away we see the huddled forms of sleeping men. Closer to us, Jesus is awake, kneeling in prayer. We look into his face and shudder. It's lined with agony from some deeper ordeal than we can imagine. "Father!" he cries, his head leaning back and his eyes lifted to the black sky. "O Father, if you're willing, take this cup from me. Yet not my will, but yours be done." The moonlight shimmers in the sweat on his brow.

Suddenly an angel kneels beside him and reaches out to him. In slow, soft strokes, the angel's hand wipes the sweat from our Savior's brow and his temples. Jesus appears strengthened. He closes his eyes and draws a deep breath. (*Luke 22:43*)

The scene fades from our sight, but we watch intently as long as we can, straining at the barest outline of our Lord praying under the olive trees. We know he was there for us. How we wish we could have helped the angel serve him. But instead, he was serving *us*.

When at last we can see no more of Gethsemane, we wipe tears from our eyes and remark to our guide that angels are great *comforters* and *servants*, bringing encouragement and strength in their hands and in their voices.

Messengers to Enlighten Us

Our guide takes us onward, increasing the speed again. "Stay with me," he urges us, "and keep listening."

So we listen. We hear the angel of the Lord call down to Abraham from heaven. He promises descendants to Abraham, "as numerous as the stars in the sky and as the sand on the seashore." (*Genesis 22:15-17*)

We hear the angel of the Lord say to the wife of Manoah, "You are barren and childless, but you will conceive and bear a son." (*Judges 13:1-5*)

Centuries later we're inside the temple in Jerusalem, where a priest applies incense to the altar in the Most Holy Place. Suddenly he sees an angel of the Lord and is gripped with fear. The angel says, "Don't be afraid, Zechariah. Your prayer has been heard. Your wife Elizabeth will bear you a son, and you're to name him John." (*Luke 1:11-13*)

With the blink of an eye we're six months forward in time. We're again in Nazareth in Galilee. A young girl is frightened by the sight of the angel Gabriel, and is troubled by his greeting. But Gabriel says, "Don't be afraid, Mary. You've found favor with God. You will be with child and give birth to a Son, and you're to name him Jesus." (*Luke 1:26-31*)

Now nine months later: We're on a hillside outside Bethlehem in Judea, where shepherds struck with fear are crouched on the ground. An angel has appeared and the glory of the Lord lights up the sky and the hill and the shepherds and the sheep. "Don't be afraid," the angel says. "I bring you good news of great joy that will be for all the people. Today in the town of David a Savior has been born to you. He is Christ the Lord." (*Luke 2:9-12*)

A lifetime later: In Jerusalem two women approach a tomb. They're shocked to see the stone rolled back from the tomb's entrance, and a white-robed angel sitting on the stone. "Don't be afraid," the angel tells the women. "I know you seek Jesus, who was crucified. He isn't here; he has risen, just as he said." (*Matthew 28:1-7*)

A quarter-century later: We're on a battered ship in a howling storm on the Mediterranean Sea. It is night. Below decks where a prisoner has been trying to sleep, an angel stands beside him. "Don't be afraid, Paul," the angel says. "You must stand trial before Caesar; and God has graciously given you the lives of all who sail with you." (*Acts 27:13-26*)

And finally, to another glimpse of the future: In the middle of the sky an angel is soaring. He has the eternal gospel to proclaim to everyone on earth. And he calls in a loud voice, "Fear God and give him glory, because the hour of his judgment has come. Worship him who made the heavens, the earth, the sea and the streams of water." *(Revelation 14:6-7)*

Yes, we tell each other—angels are *messengers* who inform and enlighten us with tidings from God.

Our journey is over. We give warm thanks to our guide for taking us on this incredible voyage through the Bible. He accepts our invitation to join us for a meal, and over a fine dinner we discuss our discoveries from the trip. We're grateful the guide has joined us because he continues to offer helpful explanations here and there, while eating heartily. During dessert you and I briefly become engrossed in comparing impressions of the soaring angel we saw at our last stop, the one who had the gospel to proclaim. Suddenly we notice the guide has disappeared. Beside his plate is a slip of paper. We pick it up and read these handwritten words in gold ink:

> *"Do not forget to entertain strangers,*
> *for by so doing some people have entertained angels*
> *without knowing it."*
> —*Hebrews 13:2*

Three Warnings

A trip like that will give anyone a healthy respect for angels. But before looking longer and closer at them, we need to get a few guidelines out on the table. These principles are key warnings that will serve us well as we move forward.

The first principle: *We must not create or reshape angels according to our own fancy.* Countless multitudes have fallen into this error. In today's spiritual smorgasbord an angel can be anything you make it out to be. A majority of the angel representations we see—in paintings and giftbooks, or as lapel pins and china figurines, or gracing a host of other varieties of merchandise—are merely the product of human imagination. The word "angel" used in marketing these items is from a totally different vocabulary than the one used in the Bible. These so-called "angels" could just as well be labeled "fairies" or "phantoms" or even "devils" and be closer to the truth.

When *Time* magazine spoke of angels as "all fluff and meringue, kind, nonjudgmental," and "available to everyone, like aspirin" — you can be certain that God's angels weren't being described, but only the modern counterfeit whose roots go no deeper than foolish fantasy, pure commercialism, or even deliberate deception.

Bestselling author Sophy Burnham (*A Book of Angels*) says that angels became popular "because we created this concept of God as punitive, jealous, judgmental," and she assures us that "angels never are. They are utterly compassionate." She must have never read the Bible, especially the book of Revelation. She's describing not God's angels, but the modern fraud. Too bad she wasn't with us on our journey.

When it comes to spiritual reality (including angels), the Bible is the only entirely reliable source of information. And the Bible gives clear depictions that pull the rug out from under the modern phonies that people call angels.

For example, whenever gender is indicated in reference to angels in the Bible, they're always masculine. Sometimes people say they've seen female angels, but the Bible never points them out. Nor do angels ever appear in Scripture as an animal or bird, as we sometimes see in angelic folklore.

According to the Bible, angels are a created class of beings and are never represented as spiritually progressed humans. In other words, humans don't evolve or transform into angels. In a children's book on angels is this quote: "Heaven is a place where girls get turned into angels and then God tries to do the best he can with the boys." But actually, sweet little girls have no more chance of becoming angels than the rowdiest boys. Likewise, imagining that a departed loved one now glides around as an angel is only a hollow comfort, and not in keeping with the pattern of God's Word.

Nor does the Bible indicate that these heavenly beings ever dwell inside human beings. There is no "angel within you," even on your best days.

There isn't the remotest hint in Scripture that angels spend time trying to earn their wings, like Clarence in the Jimmy Stewart movie *It's a Wonderful Life*. In fact, except for two classes of heavenly beings known as cherubim and seraphim, there isn't a lot of evidence in Scripture that angels even have wings. (Perhaps sometimes they do and sometimes they don't.)

Nor is there indication in the Bible that angels age — there are no "littlest angels" going through their growing-up years among the clouds. God's angels exist eternally. The angel Gabriel who appeared to Daniel was the same unchanged Gabriel who appeared more than five hundred years later to Mary the mother of Jesus, and to Zechariah the father of John the Baptist.

So I repeat: Steer clear of modern make-believe about angels, and trust only the Bible's perspective.

The second warning principle: *We must never let angels replace God in our lives.* This is a giant snare today for those who don't understand Scripture's teaching. I'm convinced that spiritual fads and tangents like those we see in angelmania are a tool of the enemy to keep us from following hard after God, as the deer pants for streams of water (Psalm 42:1).

All of us have a sense of spiritual destiny — a deep longing for eternity — placed within us by God. Long ago Paul reminded the pagan Greeks in Athens that God has even ordered human history "so that men would seek him and perhaps reach out for him and find him, though *he is not far from each one of us. For in him we live and move and have our being*" (Acts 17:27-28). But that spiritual framework and longing is easily misdirected or perverted, because our sin makes us love darkness rather than God's light. People who want a spiritual plaything or placebo are quick to bring their search for God to a dead end, and to search instead for angels.

Christianity Today warned, "Angels too easily provide a temptation for those who want a 'fix' of spirituality without bothering with God himself."

Professor Robert Ellwood, a specialist in unorthodox religions at the University of Southern California, observes, "With angels around, people feel they don't have to bother an Almighty God in order to get help."

IN THE PRESENCE OF ANGELS—Part II   53

This preference for angels over their Creator (and ours) is an insult to God. The very thought that we would have an angel's help *instead of* God's should fill us with grief, as it once did to the people of Israel. After they were rescued from Egypt but then sinned against God by making the golden calf (Exodus 32), God mentioned to Moses a new plan for the rest of Israel's trip to the Promised Land. *"I will send an angel before you,"* he said. "But I will not go with you, because you are a stiff-necked people and I might destroy you on the way" (33:1-3).

Did the Israelites jump for joy when they heard about this change in leadership for the journey? Did they consider an angel a more companionable guide than God? No. "When the people heard these distressing words, they began to mourn…" (33:4).

Tragedy awaits anyone who turns for spiritual help in any direction away from God. Whatever spiritual reality that person encounters will most likely be from Satan, who would just as soon come to the party dressed as an angel of light as anything else. A desire for angels that's greater than a desire for the Creator can only lead to trouble. An infatuation with angels can be as wrong as any other infatuation with anything except God. Angels are not the Creator; they were created by the Creator, just as food and sex and ourselves and other people were.

The Ten Commandments begin with warnings about turning away from God. It's enlightening to think how heaven's angels fit in when we go back and read the first two commandments:

> You shall have no other gods before me.
> You shall not make for yourself an idol *in the form of anything in heaven above* or on the earth beneath or in the waters below. You shall not bow down to them or worship them… (Exodus 20:3-5).

Even something as holy as an angel in heaven above is never to be turned into an idol.

That leads directly to the third warning principle: *Angels must never receive our worship.* Scripture hits this one head-on. In Colossians 2:18, Paul speaks against "anyone who delights in false humility and the worship of angels." Worshiping angels is another exhibition of the basic idolatry charged against sinful mankind in Romans 1:25 — "They exchanged the truth of God for a lie, and worshiped and served created things rather than the Creator."

One of the most devoted men of God in Scripture had to be reprimanded twice on this point. John was the apostle of love, noted for his teaching on love and his deep bond of love with Jesus. In the concluding line of his letter which we know as 1 John, he penned these words: "Dear children, keep yourselves from idols." Who would suspect that John himself would soon come up short in resisting idolatry?

Late in his life, while in exile on the island of Patmos, he was given the visions recorded in the book of Revelation, visions filled with angels throughout. After one ecstatic scene of heavenly worship at the wedding supper of the Lamb (Revelation 19), a guiding angel turned to John and asked him to write these words: "Blessed are those who are invited to the wedding supper of the Lamb!" The angel added, "These are the true words of God."

At once, John "fell at his feet *to worship him.*"

The angel's rebuke was quick: "Do not do it! I am a fellow servant with you and with your brothers who hold to the testimony of Jesus. *Worship God!*" (19:10).

But this temptation is dangerous enough that we'll see John warned about it once more. In the climax of his visions, an angel showed and described to John the heavenly New Jerusalem and its inexpressible glory. "These words are trustworthy and true," the angel said to him (22:6). John also heard Christ's promise to come soon. Then again we read John's honest account:

I, John, am the one who heard and saw these things. And when I had heard and seen them, I fell down *to worship* at the feet of the angel who had been showing them to me.

But he said to me, "Do not do it! I am a fellow servant with you and with your brothers the prophets and of all who keep the words of this book. *Worship God!*" (22:8-9)

John's weakness on this point is a good reminder of how easy it is to sin through idolatry. Worshiping angels is as wrong as giving control of our lives to anything or anyone else other than God. Angel worship is no more acceptable to God than the worship of money or power or self-indulgence. The Lord says, "You shall have *no other gods* before me."

We're to cultivate the same devotion to him that the writer of Psalm 73 attained. He could say to God, "Whom have I *in heaven* but you? And earth has nothing I desire besides you" (73:25-26). Can you pray these same words in all honesty?

Most of us find John's fall into angel-worship quite understandable. Who would not be tempted to fall down before these majestic beings, especially after seeing all that John had seen them do in Revelation. The sight of God's true angels must be awe-inspiring beyond anything we can imagine. Perhaps one reason angels are almost always invisible is so that we won't be tempted to do what John did. We're tempted enough as it is to worship the work of our own hands. What would we do if we saw angels every day?

But even if we could see them, angels pale into insignificance in relation to a glimpse of God. A. W. Tozer helps us see the comparison:

Forever God stands apart, in light unapproachable. He is as high above an archangel as above a caterpillar, for the gulf that separates the archangel from the caterpillar is but finite, while the gulf between God and the archangel is infinite. The caterpillar and the archangel, though far removed from each other in the scale of created things, are nevertheless one in that they are alike created. They both belong

in the category of that-which-is-not-God and are separated from
God by infinitude itself.

Such majestic beings as angels can help lift our eyes from this troubled
and temporal earth. But they are meant to draw our gaze to the Lord, not to
themselves. All glory is due to God, and he has no intention of sharing it
with angels. Angels deserve no more worship than caterpillars.

We, too, are spiritual beings, and as we go honestly and carefully into a
deeper study of angels, our spirits cannot help but experience the desire to
worship. So as we go on, if you remember any words at all that you've heard
angels speak in Scripture, remember especially these two:

Worship God!

Chapter Four

THE ANGELS AND GOD

W E'VE SEEN SOMETHING now of what angels do in the Bible. Impressive, I'm sure you'll agree. But you might ask, what evidence is there (and you hope there's plenty) that angels are still doing all those things today?

The right starting place for answering that question is to look closely at the character of God himself. God had his reasons for creating angels. And just like his reasons for creating you and me, those reasons spring from *who God is*.

Communication Channels

As we prepare for that closer look at God, let's first tighten up a bit our understanding of what we mean when we speak of "angels." A basic, stripped-down definition of angels is that they are spirit beings from outside this world.

Within that loose meaning are two broad categories of angels: good and bad. The good ones we call God's angels. They have always served and obeyed him, and always will. The bad ones are fallen angels — Satan and his demons. They are evil spirits who disobeyed God and continue to do so. They have a story all their own, one we can learn much from. We'll look at it later. Until we do, when we speak of "angels" here we mean only the good kind.

In the Bible, our English word "angel" translates the Hebrew word *mal'ak* in the Old Testament and the Greek word *angelos* in the New. The core meaning of both those words is *messenger.* That's the essence of who and what angels are. They are couriers for Someone other than themselves. They're Someone else's ambassadors, Someone else's agents. They represent only him, and never themselves. They are channels to carry only his information. They speak and act according to his instructions and they bear his authority.

The next time you read a Scripture passage about them, try substituting the word *messenger* for *angel* to get a good feel for this crucial aspect of their essence. Apart from God, angels can do nothing and are nothing. Their very food and drink is to do his will and accomplish his work. And God's will and work for angels is to *communicate his messages,* both by what they say and what they do.

They are *his* messengers. When they give us strength or enlightenment, it is God's strength or enlightenment that they impart. Their encouragement is God's encouragement. Their guidance is God's guidance. Their protection is God's protection. When they bring comfort, it is God's comfort they offer. And when they bring wrath, it is God's wrath they inflict.

That's why the right understanding of angels must go back to God's character. God himself is a communicator. *Word* is one of his right and proper names: "In the beginning was the Word … and the Word was God" (John 1:1). God "reveals his thoughts to man," the prophet Amos says (Amos 4:13). God makes himself known. He's always talking to you and to me. "The whole Bible supports this idea," writes A. W. Tozer:

> God is speaking. Not God spoke, but *God is speaking.* He is, by his nature, continuously articulate. He fills the world with his speaking voice.

Angels are only one of many ways he does this. He has also communicated through human messengers: "In the past God *spoke* to our forefathers *through the prophets* at many times and in various ways" (Hebrews 1:1). Our Scriptures are the living and active record of those past prophecies from God. We also hear God calling in the life of Jesus Christ: "In these last days he has *spoken* to us by his Son" (Hebrews 1:2).

Even the sky above is a 3-D screen showing God's constant communication: "The heavens *declare* the glory of God; the skies *proclaim* the work of his hands. Day after day they pour forth *speech....*" (Psalm 19:1-2). In fact the same stream of divine expression comes through unceasingly in all of nature. It's so steady and continual that those who miss the message are "without a rag of excuse," as J. B. Phillips words it in his paraphrase of Romans 1:19-20.

> It is not that they do not know the truth about God; indeed he has made it quite plain. For since the beginning of the world the invisible attributes of God, e.g., his eternal power and deity, have been plainly discernible through things which he has made....

Nature is God's mouthpiece; the design reflects the Designer. And since true science is the observation and understanding of nature, science's full and proper purpose is to point us toward God.

Angels have a wonderfully unique role in God's communication, yet their work is interwoven with these other ways in which he speaks. How we got the book of Revelation is a good picture of this. We're told that God revealed the book's message to Jesus. Jesus then revealed it to a human messenger (the apostle John), but he did it *through an angel*. Lastly, John revealed the message by recording it in the book we now read in the back of our Bibles.

So the communication sequence here was:

God → Jesus → angel → John → Scripture → you and me.

Look carefully to see if you catch all that in the opening lines of Revelation:

> The revelation of Jesus Christ, which God gave him to show his ser-
> vants.... He made it known by *sending his angel* to his servant John,
> who testifies to everything he saw — that is, the word of God and the
> testimony of Jesus Christ.

The majestic ending of Revelation makes the same point. First the angel
tells John,

> These words are trustworthy and true. The Lord, the God of the spir-
> its of the prophets, *sent his angel* to show his servants the things that
> must soon take place. (22:6)

Then we hear these words from Jesus himself:

> I, Jesus, have *sent my angel* to give you this testimony for the
> churches. I am the Root and the Offspring of David, and the bright
> Morning Star. (22:16)

As messengers, angels had a special part in giving us the Old Testament.
Both Stephen and Paul speak of the Old Testament law as being "put into
effect through angels" (Acts 7:53, Galatians 3:19), and the writer of Hebrews
calls it "the message spoken by angels" (2:2). Apparently a huge number of
angels were involved. When Moses remembers how God came to Mount
Sinai to give him the law, he says God arrived "with myriads of holy ones"
(Deuteronomy 33:2). Both *myriad* and *holy ones* are words often used in the
Bible in connection with angels. *Myriad* can mean ten thousand or simply
an exceedingly vast number, and *holy ones* reflects the purity of the angels'
devotion to God.

Angels are just as prominent in the New Testament. We'll see that especially when we study their role in the earthly life of Jesus, as well as in Revelation.

So God is always communicating in a multitude of ways, and his angels
play a big part.

Of course you and I are also communicators. So are the people you most enjoy being around. Suppose you received a letter today from a favorite friend who's far away. What would you do with it first? Would you stare at the stationery for hours, to analyze and admire it? Would you obtain a chemical analysis of the ink, to learn exactly what it's made of? Would you investigate where the paper came from, and how it was woven and cut?

No — paper and ink are simply the means of your friend's communication. What you're interested in is your *friend* and your friend's *message*. The paper and ink fully serve their intended purpose by simply bringing that personal message to you.

The same logic applies in our approach to angels. Angels are just a means of communication from the God who communicates. Through what angels say and do, God personally expresses his friendship to us and his fatherhood and much more. What's important is the message angels bring — not the messengers themselves.

To a Deeper Love for Christ

Remember, however, that angels are always *one-way* messengers. They are God's messengers to us, and never our messengers to God. No one in Scripture ever prays to an angel, and neither should we. They are not go-betweens or mediators between us and heaven.

They are not mediators because there is Another who already fulfills that role — and praise God for that! "For there is one God and *one mediator* between God and men, *the man Christ Jesus*" (1 Timothy 2:5) Christ's mediation brings us what any mediation of angels could never begin to accomplish: the freedom and eternal salvation of our souls. "Christ is the mediator of a new covenant, that those who are called may receive the promised eternal inheritance — now that he has died as a ransom to set them free" (Hebrews 9:15).

That's why in the New Testament the mention of angels is so completely dominated by a focus on the excellence of Christ in every way.

Now that angels have been on our minds so much, this New Testament focus is a perfect stimulus for letting angels lead us to a deeper love for Christ. Come along with me through a few of these angel passages, and keep asking yourself: How well does my own devotion and esteem for Christ and his gospel match up with what's being taught here?

Paul is so struck by Christ's unconquerable love that by comparison he lumps angels together with demons, as well as "anything else in all creation." He exclaims that none of these "will be able to separate us from the love of God that is *in Christ Jesus* our Lord" (Romans 8:38-39).

Paul's commitment to the gospel of Christ is great enough that by contrast he is ready to invoke a curse upon angels. Listen to his intensity:

> But even if we or *an angel from heaven* should preach a gospel other than the one we preached to you, let him be eternally condemned! As we have already said, so now I say again: If anybody is preaching to you a gospel other than what you accepted, let him be eternally condemned! (Galatians 1:8)

If you think such a harsh attitude toward angels is too extreme, remember that Paul is willing to apply the same curse to himself (as well as to "anybody" else) if ever he should fail to stay true to Christ's gospel. Absolutely everything is at stake in our answer to the good news. To be right with God through Christ is heaven; by comparison, to be right only with an angel is hell.

Paul proclaims how God raised Christ and seated him "in the heavenly realms, far above *all rule and authority, power and dominion*" (Ephesians 1:20-21). In those heavenly realms he surely had in view the glorious ranks of angels — powerful and stately, yet so very far below Christ.

When Paul tells us to set our minds and hearts "on things above" in Colossians 3:1-2, he points out specifically that heaven is "where Christ is." Angels are there too, but Paul doesn't put them in the spotlight. It's Christ who can make us heavenly minded, not angels. When Paul later warns against worshiping angels, in the same breath he reminds us that "reality…is found *in Christ*" (Colossians 1:17-18).

In Philippians 2:9-10 he tells us that God exalted Christ

> to the highest place and gave him the name that is above every name, that at the name of Jesus every knee should bow, *in heaven* and on earth and under the earth.

Angels, men, and demons must all alike bend the knee someday to acknowledge the glory and supremacy of Jesus. (Have you done so today?)

The most extensive treatment of angels in the entire Bible stretches over the first two chapters in the book of Hebrews. But the whole discussion makes one resounding point—Christ is utterly superior to angels. With reason after reason, the author drives his message home:

- God calls Jesus his Son, a title angels never wear. (1:4-5)
- God commands angels to worship Jesus. (1:6)
- God gives Jesus a solid eternal throne from which to rule as King, while the work of angels is like fleeting breezes or flickering flames. (1:7-8)
- Jesus knows more gladness than angels. God set him high above his companions (the angels) by anointing him with "the oil of joy." (1:9)
- Jesus himself created the world—a temporal world with an appointed end. Meanwhile he himself stays unchanged and eternal, highly honored by God, and with all his enemies crouched underfoot. Angels, on the other hand, are only servant spirits whose job is to wait upon the human beings rescued from that temporal world. (1:10-14)
- In the world to come it isn't angels who'll be in charge, but Jesus. (2:5-9)

On this foundation the author of Hebrews moves on to a more subtle point in the heart of chapter 2. It dawns on us with breathtaking fitness. The author has earlier stated that angels are spirits, and are like wind and fire.

Now he reminds us that Jesus for a short time was made "a little lower than the angels" — he embodied himself in human form. He who is eternal Spirit was instead given "flesh and blood" like men and women, and in so doing "he shared in their humanity." He was made "like" us — "in every way."

It was in that human body that "he suffered when he was tempted."

And it was in that body that he would "taste death."

As spirits, angels cannot bleed or die. Christ could, and did — for you and for me.

And for you and for me, it's that distinction between Christ and angels that makes an eternity of difference. For by it, Christ was able "to destroy him who holds the power of death — that is, the devil" (2:14).

Angel Stairway

But don't let me mislead you into writing angels off. All this discussion is not to put down angels, but to exalt Christ. And that's a necessary step. Nothing in all creation can truly be understood aright until seen in proper relationship to Christ. Exalting Jesus will not make us shrug off angels. No, it will allow us to really comprehend angels, and to actually receive their best help.

One more sketch from Scripture will help root this rich perspective of Christ and the angels even deeper in our hearts. Remember the dream the man Jacob had the night he slept on the ground with a rock for his pillow? In that dream

> he saw a stairway resting on the earth, with its top reaching to heaven, and *the angels of God were ascending and descending on it.* There above it stood the Lord. (Genesis 28:12-13)

Nineteen centuries later, near the Jordan River, Jesus was having a first conversation with a few men who someday would be his apostles to the world. "I tell you the truth," he told them, "you shall see heaven open, and *the angels of God ascending and descending on the Son of man*" (John 1:51). His words would easily bring to their minds Jacob's dream. But instead of a stairway, Christ spoke of himself. What did he mean?

Perhaps the meaning of our Lord's words will not come fully alive until we see him return from heaven "in his glory, and all the angels with him" (Matthew 25:31). But in the interplay between those Scriptures in John and Genesis, John Calvin found this clue: "that it is solely by the intercession of Christ that the ministry of angels extends to us."

Even now angels may come and go between heaven and earth only by way of Christ. Solely in obedience to his will are they sent to serve us. His own ministry to us, his plans for us, and his protection of us are the busy stairway they use in their daily diligence of attending to our needs.

Lord of Heaven's Armies

God is the Great Communicator, speaking to us through Christ, through whom also the angels are sent to serve us. God sends the angels to show us his love for us, and his power.

To help us understand this he identifies with angels in a special way — through one of his names.

More than 250 times in the Bible, God calls himself "the Lord of Hosts," meaning "the Lord of Heavenly Armies." The Hebrew term is *Yahweh Seba'ot*. Occasionally in the King James Version it's given as "Lord Sabaoth." Many modern English translations render the name as "the Lord Almighty" to rightly help us focus on the power it implies — God sovereignly commands all the forces of heaven. But perhaps a little is lost in that translation. Keeping the word "hosts" brings quicker to mind the innumerable and powerful angels who make up heaven's armies. It's as if God wants us to envision those robust ranks of troops whenever we hear him called by that name.

This name instantly gives us a royal and military picture of the Lord leading his celestial soldiers. One day soon we'll surely think of this name again and shout it in praise "when the Lord Jesus is revealed from heaven in blazing fire with his powerful angels" (2 Thessalonians 1:7).

Interestingly enough, this name for God seems to be used most often in Old Testament books where overt angelic activity is less prominent. It's as if God wanted his people to especially remember the angels at his instant command even when these heavenly beings weren't being seen or heard from.

In the New Testament the Greek version of the name "Lord of Hosts" is used in James 5:4 in a frightful warning to the rich who hoard their wealth. This passage, too, looks ahead to the time of Christ's return with his angels. But notice how it recalls the judgment and wrath they will bring, rather than redemption:

> Look! The wages you failed to pay the workmen who mowed your fields are crying out against you. The cries of the harvesters have reached the ears of the *Lord of Hosts*. You have lived on earth in luxury and self-indulgence. You have fattened yourselves in *the day of slaughter.*

The appearance of the Lord and his fighting forces will be overwhelming enough for everyone, but a terrifying sight indeed for the wicked. Until then, he wants us all to bear the picture in mind.

With all the evil occurring today, it's easy to wonder if God has lost control. If this world is going to hell in a handbasket, can't somebody do something about it? But even in times of apparent chaos, the Lord of Hosts is still in charge. The Lord of the Armies is still the Sovereign God, the ultimate Victor, our Captain of Salvation. And he and I are on the same side. That gives me comfort.

At the same time it inspires in me a great reverence, which is something the angels won't let us forget.

Both Near and Far Away

When you ponder angels in Scripture you quickly lock in on two things: majesty and awe. The majesty is always there in who they are, and the awe is constantly inspired in the people who are exposed to them.

THE ANGELS AND GOD   67

We know the source of this is not the angels themselves, but God. His majesty and his capacity to inspire awe far surpass theirs. His glory is exalted *"above the heavens,"* the psalmist announces. "Who is like the Lord our God, the One who sits enthroned on high, who *stoops down to look on the heavens and the earth?"* (Psalm 113:4-6). In a real sense God looks downward even upon heaven where the angels are. They, too, are merely his creation.

In fact, the more we think about it, the more we experience two separate and conflicting reactions to this image of God as the Lord of Hosts, the Lord of angel armies. We're glad to think of such powerful help available on our behalf. What a privilege it is that God would come down from heaven and intervene for us.

But just to visualize such a scene of holy splendor and unearthly force only emphasizes our own smallness and weakness and unworthiness. Suddenly, with more clarity than ever, we can see how much mightier and holier he is than we've imagined. He's so different and distant from us.

Yes, he comes — but even in his coming, he creates a bigger gap. We see how close God draws, but also how far apart from us he remains. He's always near, yet always far. It's a mystery to our souls!

The angels only accent the paradox. How gracious and thrilling it is that they come to us with the Lord's messages, opening a window for us into God and his heaven. Yet the very sight of them causes even the best of people to shrink back in fear, thinking only of the great gulf between God and themselves.

Isaiah is one of those who had that experience, and his account of it is one of the most awesome passages in Scripture.

It was "in the year that King Uzziah died" (6:1). The long, eventful reign of that remarkable monarch had come to an end. But Isaiah got a glimpse of a greater King. He says he saw "the Lord seated on a throne, high and exalted."

Above him, Isaiah saw glorious angelic beings called seraphs. These seraphs had to cover their faces with their wings, for even they could not gaze straight at God's glory. Isaiah heard them calling, "Holy, holy, holy is the Lord of Hosts." They gave triple emphasis to the fact that God is separate and set apart over all else. Theologians like to call this God's "transcendence." He is holy and high and exalted, forever above and beyond and outside all his creation.

And yet Isaiah also heard these seraphs cry out, "The whole earth is full of his glory." Somehow this Holy God is also actively present in all of his creation. This is what theologians call God's "immanence."

Both God's transcendence and his immanence are always true at the same time. In our limited human thinking we tend to lean first one way and then the other as we think about God. But in reality the two are always in perfect balance — he is always near, and he is always far.

> "Am I only a God nearby," declares the Lord, "and not a God far away? Can anyone hide in secret places so that I cannot see him?" declares the Lord. "Do not I fill heaven and earth?" declares the Lord. (Jeremiah 23:23-24)

Paul instructed the wise men in the marketplace of Athens on the same point: "The God who made the world and everything in it is *the Lord of heaven and earth*," he said, "and does not live in temples built by hands." God is above and beyond all that. But this same God, Paul went on to say, *"is not far* from each one of us. For in him we live and move and have our being" (Acts 17:22-28).

Angels, too, come near, and yet also keep their distance. They're like that because of the One who created them and who designs their work. They can be as winsome as serving baked bread to Elijah or helping Daniel to his feet. They can be as repellent as a flaming sword to shut out man and woman from their perfect garden.

So — back to this chapter's original question: Today, do angels still do all that the Bible shows them doing in the past?

I see no biblical reason why they cannot and will not, because God has not changed. He still communicates. He is near to us. He is our Savior and our loving Father. 'He who did not spare his own Son, but gave him up for us all — how will he not also, along with him, graciously give us *all things?*" (Romans 8:32). Surely that "all things" must include angels.

But their services can never be summoned by you or me, and their presence can never be predicted. They're as near as they've ever been, but they're also just as far away.

It's a mystery. In fact, mystery saturates this whole topic. But mystery is good and healthy for us, and maybe more now than ever. So many Christians today are lacking in awe and a sense of mystery when they consider the things of God. We think we have as much of him figured out as is practical and approachable—and isn't the rest only small potatoes anyway? My prayer is that this presumption will start to be corrected as we gain respect for the secrets surrounding God's angels.

God hasn't told us everything about them, and never will. Even what he *has* revealed can't be entirely comprehended by us, because of our mental and spiritual limitations. But the treasures he has shown us are there to be discovered and possessed. "The secret things belong to the Lord our God, but the things revealed belong to us and to our children forever" (Deuteronomy 29:29).

Chapter Five

WHAT ANGELS ARE

WHAT EXACTLY *are* angels, anyway? What are they made of, where did they come from, where do they stay? How are they like me? How are they different? If an angel should appear — if I should somehow become acquainted with one — what should I expect?

With so much misinformation accumulating today on the subject of angels, let's go back and begin where the Bible begins.

Angels are first of all *created beings* — like you and me, and like caterpillars, as we noted earlier. They are not the result of the Big Bang. They did not come about in the hierarchy of some evolutionary process. God made angels.

And just like you and me and the caterpillar, angels were made *in* Christ and *through* Christ and *for* Christ. In Colossians 1:16 we read that *"all things were created"* with those same intricate connections to God the Son. Christ was the *cause* of all created things, he was the *way* and the *means* in which they were fashioned, and he is the *purpose* for their very existence. For all created things, he is the *where from*, he is the *how*, and he is the *why*. Christ is their King and Master, just as he is ours.

But is there any reason to believe Paul was thinking beyond earthly creation in this passage? Did he really have angels in mind, any more than caterpillars?

Evidently so. In the same verse Paul rushes into an overview of what he's including:

> ...things *in heaven* and on earth, visible and *invisible,* whether thrones or powers or rulers or authorities; *all things* were created by him [by Christ], and for him.

In this deeply bonded created order, Paul takes care to include what is heavenly and invisible. Those characteristics definitely fit angels, as we'll soon see. Paul's purpose in including them here may well have been to counter the spread of angel worship in the Colossian church which he refers to later (2:18). He knew that a focus on Christ is the corrective for all drifting.

Angels apparently have no problem going astray by worshiping each other. They know better. They know they were created only by the Lord's will and pleasure. Angelic beings themselves declare this while worshiping God in Revelation 4.

> They lay their crowns before the throne and say:
> "You are worthy, our Lord and God,
>   to receive glory and honor and power,
> for *you created all things,*
>   and by your will they were created
>   and have their being."

In those last four words these angelic creations confess a further truth: Only by God's will and pleasure does their existence continue even now. This, too, is as true of us as of angels: Why we were born is the same reason as why we're still kept alive, and that reason is wrapped up in the will and pleasure of God.

This foundational fact demands one simple response above all: praise to God. Psalm 148 begins by calling on everything in the "heavens" and "the heights above"—specifically including sun, moon, stars, *and angels*—to give God praise. "Let them praise the name of the Lord, *for he commanded and they were created.*" This, too, is as true for us as for angels and stars. The angels and stars are continually and joyfully meeting this requirement of praise. How about you?

Created for Us

But *why* would God create these troops of heavenly messengers when he certainly doesn't need them? As Calvin says, "Whenever he pleases, he passes them by, and performs his own work by a single nod."

So Calvin comes to this conclusion: In creating angels, God must have had *our* interests in mind. God employs angels simply as "a help to our weakness," in order to "elevate our hopes or strengthen our confidence."

Calvin admits that God's offer of his own personal protection ought to be enough for us. He says it's "improper" for us "still to look round for help." He adds, however, that if God in his "infinite goodness and indulgence" chooses to provide angels for our weakness, "it would ill become us to overlook the favor."

His conclusion reflects the teaching of Hebrews 1:14, a verse we keep coming back to: Angels are "ministering spirits sent to serve those who will inherit salvation." Angels are here for us.

Angels aren't named in the creation account in Genesis 1, where the narrative focuses on visible creation. Their omission in that passage could be another indication that angels are not under human authority. In the climax of creation week, God gave mankind the privilege and responsibility of ruling "over the fish of the sea and the birds of the air, over the livestock, over all the earth, and over all the creatures that move along the ground" (Genesis 1:26). But that list doesn't include angels. We can herd cattle and cage canaries and grow cantaloupe and cauliflower in our gardens, but we can't make angels do our laundry or warm up the car.

Created in the Beginning

When did God create angels?

The Lord told Job that angels were already on the scene to celebrate when the earth was created. He asks Job in 38:4, "Where were you when I laid the earth's foundation?" Job, of course, wasn't around, so for his benefit God adds a few details of what that ground-breaking was like: It was "while the morning stars sang together and all the angels shouted for joy" (38:7). Job wasn't there when the earth was formed, but the angels were, and having a good time of it too.

Therefore angels were made apparently before the third day of the creation week, the day when God gathered waters into seas and the dry land appeared (Genesis 1:9-10).

Psalm 104 seems to reflect the same timing for the angels' appearance. It's a psalm praising God's greatness for how he made and sustains all creation. In richly poetic imagery, the opening lines give a broad overview of what God created. The psalm seems to follow the same sequence as in Genesis 1: first of all light, then the heavens and the gathering of heavenly waters, then the land, seas, animals, and man.

Coming along naturally in this procession is verse four which reads, "He makes winds his messengers, flames of fire his servants." These lines often are taken as referring to angels. That's the way the New Testament writer quotes them in Hebrews 1:7. And in Psalm 104, this reference to angels comes immediately before the first mention of the earth in verse five: "He set the earth on its foundations."

Creation scientist Dr. Henry Morris, my good friend and a member of our church, said he believed angels were formed on the second day of creation. He pointed to Psalm 104 and its implication that angels came as "the next act after the creation of the space-time cosmos and the establishment of God's light-arrayed throne therein." Very likely the angels are older than anything in the world as we see it.

Has God created any more angels since then? I have no biblical reason to believe he has. And apparently there's been no reduction in their number either (except for the dismissal of the fallen angels, which we'll take up later). Nor has there been any increase, since angels don't reproduce — according to Jesus' statement that angels don't marry (Matthew 22:30, Mark 12:25, Luke 20:34-36). We have as many angels today as we've ever had.

Angels Are Innumerable

And exactly how many angels is that?

No precise count is given in Scripture, but there's plenty of evidence that they make up a mighty multitude.

On that dark night of agony when an angel came to minister to the Son of God as he prayed in Gethsemane, Jesus had to stop his disciples from fighting against soldiers who came to arrest him. Christ admonished his men with these words: "Do you think I cannot call on my Father, and he will at once put at my disposal more than twelve legions of angels?" (Matthew 26:53). That's enough for each disciple to have his own entire legion for his personal bodyguards. A typical Roman legion numbered from three to six thousand men, often with the same number of backup troops. So the total host Jesus brought to mind would be as great as 144,000 heavenly soldiers.

In a majestic and timeless picture in Hebrews 12:22, we're told that we've come to *"thousands upon thousands* of angels in joyful assembly." In various English translations this assembly is called "the gathering of *countless* happy angels," or *"innumerable* angels in festal gathering," or *"millions* of angels gathered for the festival." Here again is a form of the Greek word *myriad,* the word we saw earlier with a meaning of ten thousand or a vast number.

In Psalm 68:17, David probably is thinking of angelic warriors when he says, "The chariots of God are *tens of thousands and thousands of thousands.*"

In one of Daniel's visions in Babylon, he saw God (whom he called "the Ancient of Days") on a flaming throne surrounded by angelic beings: "*Thousands upon thousands* attended him; *ten thousand times ten thousand* stood before him" (Daniel 7:10).

The same language is echoed in John's vision of God's throne in Revelation 5:11.

> Then I looked and heard the voice of many angels, numbering *thousands upon thousands, and ten thousand times ten thousand.* They encircled the throne....

Taken literally, "ten thousand times ten thousand" angels would be a hundred million of them. That's enough to fill the California Angels' baseball stadium in Anaheim for every home game for nearly twenty years, without anyone going back a second time.

In using such numbers the Scriptures are probably describing simply an inexpressibly large host, far more angels than any of us could look at and count. That's not to say *God* doesn't know their number. The Scriptures say he's counted the hairs on our head (Matthew 10:30). And he's numbered and named all the stars (Psalm 147:4) and knows that "not one of them is missing" (Isaiah 40:26). If he's calculated totals for the stars and our hair, he surely has the angels tallied.

Since a certain portion of the angels became fallen angels along with Satan, some Bible scholars have speculated that perhaps every place in heaven vacated by a fallen angel will be filled in eternity by a redeemed human being. That would bring heaven's population back to its original number when the angels were first formed.

Angels Are Heavenly

Angels — the good angels, that is — definitely call God's heaven their home. We see this especially in the gospels and the book of Revelation. The one who ministered to Jesus while he prayed in Gethsemane is called "an angel *from heaven*" (Luke 22:43). Three days later an angel "came down *from heaven*" to roll back the stone guarding his tomb (Matthew 28:2). Jesus himself refers often to "angels *in heaven*" (Matthew 18:10, 22:30, 24:36). The angels who announced his birth are called "the *heavenly* host" (Luke 2:13), and when they left the shepherds they returned "into *heaven*" (2:15).

Heaven is their dwelling place because angels belong exclusively to God. The best definition of heaven is that it's God's dwelling place. "*Heaven is my throne,*" God says in Isaiah 66:1, and that is where angels work and live. If you tend to picture angels going through life lounging on fluffy clouds or cruising from star to star, you've missed a big truth. They inhabit the throne-room of God, because they belong to God.

Jesus specifically referred to them as *God's* angels (Luke 12:8-9, 15:10). He promised the disciples that when they saw "heaven open," they would also see "the angels *of God*" ascending and descending on himself (John 1:51).

Because Jesus is God, he also referred to the angels as belonging to himself, especially when he spoke of his return to earth and his coming judgment (Matthew 13:41, 16:27, 24:31).

The holy angels — the good angels — belong only to the God of the Bible, and therefore to his heaven. They do not belong to earth or to any earthly religion or philosophy.

Angels Are Spirit Beings

Someone once asked me, "Do you know why angels can fly?" I said, "No. Why?" He answered, "Because they take themselves lightly."

In a way he's right. Angels are spirit beings, without permanent material bodies to haul around. They are specifically called "*ministering spirits*" (Hebrews 1:14).

So each angel is a *spirit*. But what does that mean?

A. W. Tozer defines the word this way:

Spirit means existence on a level above and beyond matter; it means
life subsisting in another mode. Spirit is substance that has no
weight, no dimension, no size nor extension in space. These quali-
ties belong to matter and can have no application to spirit. Yet spirit
has true being and is objectively real.

Angels are real, but without material substance as we think of it. They
apparently have no physical nature, no breath or blood. If they occupy some
form of permanent bodies, these would be spiritual bodies, perhaps like the
ones we'll wear someday in eternity (1 Corinthians 15:44). The angels do
not marry, as we saw earlier from Jesus' words, and do not procreate.

You and I are spiritual beings too. But unlike angels, we're also physical
beings. And unfortunately, here on earth our physical nature tends to overshadow our spiritual nature.

It must be their spiritual nature — as well as their spiritual holiness —
that allows angels the continual proximity to God they enjoy, for in this they
are like God. Jesus said, "God is spirit, and his worshipers must worship in
spirit and in truth" (John 4:24).

Spirit Beings — Yet Limited

But we can't assume that the spiritual nature of angels is identical to God's
spiritual nature. Some theologians even say that although angels don't have
material bodies in comparison to man, they *do* have material bodies in comparison to God, for God's self-existent spirituality is on such a higher level
than theirs. Here we come again to more mystery surrounding angels.

In their spiritual state, angels have many limitations that God can never
have. For example, angels cannot be in more than one place at once, unlike
God, who is everywhere at once. Only God is infinite in his whereabouts;
he is *omnipresent*. David's awe-struck confession to God in Psalm 139 is that
no matter where he went or imagined himself to go, *"You* are there."

Angels are also limited in knowledge. Jesus said the angels don't know the time of his second coming to the world, and that this was knowledge even he himself did not possess while on earth (Matthew 24:36, Mark 13:32). But God in heaven always knows "the end from the beginning," and can communicate his plans to whomever he chooses (Isaiah 46:10). He is *omniscient*, all-knowing, infinite in knowledge.

Angels are also limited in power, though their power is indeed staggering to behold. In Revelation 7:1, we see how only four of them can stand and hold back destructive winds ready to rip across the earth. Three times in Revelation John says he saw a *"mighty* angel." The one in 18:21 "picked up a boulder the size of a large millstone and threw it into the sea."

The force of the angels in unleashing destruction and violence is especially evident in Revelation as Christ opens the seven seals. In case you hear of anyone rejecting this destructive picture because it's inconsistent with Jesus' teachings on peace and gentleness and love, point out to them that as Christ opens these seals, he's always described as "the Lamb." People who like soft, delicate angels are usually after a soft, delicate God as well. God is never that way, however, and neither are his heavenly servants.

But powerful as angels are, they are not all-powerful like God. They have no force of their own, and are impotent without God. They can exercise only the energy God channels through them. They operate within the divine allowance that A. W. Tozer describes so carefully:

> God has delegated power to his creatures, but being self-sufficient, he cannot relinquish anything of his perfections and, power being one of them, he has never surrendered the least iota of his power. He gives but he does not give away. All that he gives remains his own and returns to him again. Forever he must remain what he has forever been, the Lord God *omnipotent*.

As Jesus stood before Pilate awaiting the sentence of crucifixion, he told the governor, "You would have no power over me if it were not given you from above" (John 19:11). The same is as true of angels as of men. Angels would have no power if it were not given them from above. And what they have been given is limited.

Angels can face struggles. The angel who spoke with Daniel mentioned being "detained" by an encounter with what was apparently a demonic ruler, and he said the angel Michael "came to help me." Apparently this angel needed the archangel Michael's assistance to overcome the evil power he met.

God, and God alone, is infinite in power. The angel Gabriel said it best: "*Nothing* is impossible with God" (Luke 1:37).

Another mystery is how the holiness of angels is also limited and lesser than God's. We see this in the fact that some angels fell along with Satan from their original state of goodness. But God will always be perfectly holy, just, righteous, and loving. He is infinite in goodness. "Taste and see that the Lord is good" (Psalm 34:8). Jesus tells us, "Your heavenly Father is perfect" (Matthew 5:48).

In a dramatic scene in Revelation 5 we glimpse the limitation of angels in both power and holiness. Angels in splendor are circled around God's throne. God himself holds in his right hand the scroll with writing on both sides, sealed with the seven seals. A "mighty angel" shouts, "Who is worthy to break the seals and open the scroll?" Surely one of the majestic angels would be deserving of this task. "But *no one in heaven or on earth or under the earth* could open the scroll or even look inside it." Only the Lamb — Jesus Christ — is worthy of that. Angels were no more worthy of this honor than you or I, or the inhabitants of hell.

Spirit Beings — Like Wind

Angels are described in Scripture as being like "winds" and like "flames of fire" (Psalm 104:4, Hebrews 1:7). Wind and fire may be the best things on earth to help us picture the spiritual make-up of angels.

The word *wind* brings to mind their spiritual nature. In both Hebrew and Greek the words for "spirit" can also mean "breath" or "wind." And even when the words are translated "wind" as the Bible describes some breeze or storm, it's easy to imagine that maybe angels had something to do with it.

Sometimes the connection is stated and obvious, as in David's Psalm 18. He writes this about God sending angelic beings (called cherubim) to his rescue:

> He parted the heavens and came down;
>> dark clouds were under his feet.
> He mounted the cherubim and flew;
>> he soared on the wings of the *wind*.

David saw the wind and the angels together.

A thousand years later, Jesus told Nicodemus, "The *wind* blows wherever it pleases. You hear its sound, but you cannot tell where it comes from or where it is going" (John 3:8).

Then Jesus added, "So it is with everyone born of the Spirit." To that we might also add, "So it is with the angels." For angels are already spiritual beings attuned to God, and in at least that sense we become like them when we're born again.

Many Old Testament passages describe strong winds blowing on the day of God's judgment. These verses anticipate the judgment passages in Revelation, where angels are so active in accomplishing God's wrath. Remember how powerful we saw them in this work? In the verses below, think about angel power and see if you can imagine God sending angels to do the "blowing":

> When you cry out for help,
>> let your collection of idols save you!
> The *wind* will carry all of them off,
>> a mere breath will blow them away.

But the man who makes me his refuge
  will inherit the land and possess my holy mountain.
  (God's words in Isaiah 57:13)

Oh, the raging of many nations…!
Oh, the uproar of the peoples…!
Although the peoples roar like the roar of surging waters,
  when he rebukes them they flee far away,
driven before the *wind* like chaff on the hills,
  like tumbleweed before a gale.
In the evening, sudden terror!
  Before the morning, they are gone! (Isaiah 17:12-14)

The Lord will dry up
  the gulf of the Egyptian sea;
with a *scorching wind* he will sweep his hand
  over the Euphrates River. (Isaiah 11:15)

At that time this people and Jerusalem will be told, "A *scorching wind*
from the barren heights in the desert blows toward my people….
Now I pronounce my judgments against them." (Jeremiah 4:11-12)

This is what the Sovereign Lord says: In my wrath I will unleash a
violent wind, and in my anger hailstones and torrents of rain will fall
with destructive fury. (Ezekiel 13:13)

Perhaps an angel worked up the storm that sent Jonah overboard and
into a big fish's mouth: "The Lord sent a *great wind* on the sea, and such a
violent storm arose that the ship threatened to break up" (Jonah 4:8).

It's even possible that the Holy Spirit commanded angels to provide the
great noise heard on the birthday of the church — the day of Pentecost —
when "a sound like the blowing of a *violent wind* came *from heaven*" (Acts
2:2).

We don't know for certain that angels were involved in all these situations, but it isn't hard to see how they could be.

Spirit Beings — Like Fire

"Flames of fire" are the other image we get of angels in Psalm 104 and Hebrews 1. Angels are connected with flames often enough in Scripture that you may want to pack along a fire extinguisher while we explore a few of these passages. Notice in how many different ways their fire is manifested.

You'll remember how the cherubim who guarded the gates of Eden were accompanied by "a flaming sword flashing back and forth."

Later, the angel of the Lord appeared to Moses "in flames of fire from within a bush" (Exodus 3:2).

The angel of God asked Gideon to prepare a sacrifice of meat and unleavened bread, and to set it on a rock. When the angel touched the tip of his staff to the sacrifice, "fire flared from the rock, consuming the meat and the bread. And the angel of the Lord disappeared" (Judges 6:20-21).

Manoah and his wife (the parents of Samson) were visited by an angel, and Manoah also offered a sacrifice on a rock that was then consumed by fire. "As the fire blazed up from the altar toward heaven, the angel of the Lord ascended in the flame" (Judges 13:19-21).

Isaiah saw a seraph flying toward him "with a live coal in his hand" (Isaiah 6:6).

The appearance of the cherubim whom Ezekiel saw "was like burning coals of fire or like torches. Fire moved back and forth among the creatures; it was bright, and lightning flashed out of it" (Ezekiel 1:13).

The angel that overwhelmed Daniel on the banks of the Tigris River had a face "like lightning" and eyes "like flaming torches" (Daniel 10:4-6).

In John's vision he saw an angel with "legs...like fiery pillars" (Revelation 10:1).

Perhaps one of the busiest creatures in heaven is the one John mentions in Revelation 14:18 — "another angel, who *had charge of the fire....*"

Where do the angels get all that fire?

From God, of course. "Our God is a *consuming fire*" (Hebrews 12:29). When the Lord met with Moses on Mount Sinai, it was "covered with smoke, because the Lord descended on it *in fire*" (Exodus 19:18). His fire gets our attention, so we'll listen: "Our God comes and will not be silent; *a fire devours* before him" (Psalm 50:3). The Lord once promised to be *"a wall of fire"* around his people (Zechariah 2:5). And now we look forward to the time "when the Lord Jesus is revealed from heaven *in blazing fire* with his powerful angels" (2 Thessalonians 1:7).

We associate fire with hell, and frequently think of flames as the devil's instrument. But hell is set afire by God and his angels, who will toss both Satan and all who belong to him into the torturing flames of "the lake of burning sulfur" (Revelation 20:10,15). Jesus speaks of "the eternal fire prepared for the devil and his angels" (Matthew 25:41). Hell's fire isn't something Satan devised for human beings; God prepared it for Satan.

Isaiah 66:15-16 gives a good preview of the coming fiery judgment. Here as in other Scriptures, the reference to "chariots" is probably a picture of angels. We see them associated once more with both wind and fire:

> See, the Lord is coming with *fire,*
>> and his chariots are like a *whirlwind;*
> he will bring down his anger with fury,
>> and his rebuke with *flames of fire.*
> For with *fire* and with his sword
>> the Lord will execute judgment upon all men,
>> and many will be those slain by the Lord.

Fire is God's tool, and he makes it the property of angels.

Spirit Beings — Like Stars

Yes, angels are spirit beings. But since they're called "flames of fire" and since Scripture sometimes associates angels with stars, is all this a hint that the substance of angels is more like that of stars — orbs of fire — than anything else?

That's a possibility put forward by my friend Henry Morris, who said,

> This concept is beyond our naturalistic comprehension, but that is no reason for us to reject or spiritualize it prematurely. We do not know the nature of angels. Man was made of the natural chemical elements and is therefore subject to the electromagnetic and gravitational forces which control these elements. But angels are not so bound. They can fly swiftly from God's throne to earth when God commands them and they are not limited by gravity or other natural forces.

Maybe he's on to something there. Often people today who report sighting an angel have described it in terms of a brilliant light or a luminescence they couldn't describe and had never seen before.

Certainly angels in Scripture are often associated with bright light. The angels at Jesus' tomb had "clothes that gleamed like lightning" (Luke 24:4). The angel that Cornelius saw wore "shining clothes" (Acts 10:30). When an angel came to get Peter out of jail, "a light shone in the cell" (Acts 12:7). In Revelation we read of an angel whose "face was like the sun" (10:1), and about seven angels dressed in "shining linen" (15:6).

It appears to be this particular aspect of angelic demeanor — their shining brilliance — that Satan tries to counterfeit. For Paul warns us that "Satan himself masquerades as an angel *of light*" (2 Corinthians 11:14). But as with their flame, so it is with their light — it's safe to say that whatever the glow surrounding angels, it comes straight from the light of God. When the angel appeared to Bethlehem shepherds to announce Christ's birth, "the *glory of the Lord* shone around them, and they were terrified" (Luke 2:9). It was the Lord's glory that was shining, not the angel's glory. Satan can never duplicate this. Only God's holy angels are truly "angels of light."

Now back to the stars. Take a look at a few places in Scripture where the angels are associated specifically with stars. Earlier we looked at Job 38:7, where God mentions angels looking on when he laid "earth's foundation"—

> ...while the morning stars sang together
>   and all the angels shouted for joy...

If this refers to the third day of creation, then "the morning stars" could not be the lights we see in a clear night sky, since these weren't created until the fourth day. Instead it's more likely that "stars" here is another designation for the angels, joyfully singing over the works of God.

John says that in his vision,

> I saw a *star* that had fallen from the sky to the earth. The star was given the key to the shaft of the Abyss. When he opened the Abyss, smoke rose from it like the smoke from a gigantic furnace. (Revelation 9:1-2)

This star is generally interpreted as another of the angels in Revelation who are part of God's final, awful disclosure of his wrath against evil.

In Israel's war with the Canaanites, one dramatic battle against the commander Sisera was won only by supernatural intervention (Judges 4:15). After the battle, one line in Deborah's victory song goes like this:

> From the heavens *the stars fought,*
>   from their courses they fought against Sisera. (5:20)

Perhaps this is a hint of warrior angels who assisted in the battle.

It could be that even the miraculous star that brought the wise men to Bethlehem was in actuality an angel, faithfully serving God in his appointed task of guiding worshipers to the newborn King.

Stars and Angels and Us

It's easy to imagine a peaceful scene for David in the Psalms in which the stars reminded him of angels. Perhaps he was lying on his back out on a hillside one clear night near his home in Bethlehem. (Maybe it was the same hill where shepherds would hear good news from an angel a thousand years later.)

As David looked up, inspiration came to him for a new song, a song that would someday become our Psalm 8.

First David sang his praise to God, whom he could imagine far out of sight, at a distance even beyond the stars:

> O Lord, our Lord,
>> how majestic is your name in all the earth!
> You have set your glory
> *above the heavens.*

His voice continued ringing in a river of words as he addressed a searching question to God:

> When I consider your heavens, the work of your fingers,
>> the moon and the stars, which you have set in place,
> *what is man* that you are mindful of him,
>> the son of man that you care for him?

David had his mind on man, even as he gazed at the star-host shining from horizon to horizon. They made him think of angels — heavenly beings who were above him like the stars, and yet not so very far.

In the song's next line, he added another thought about man:

> You made him a little lower than the heavenly beings
>> and crowned him with glory and honor.

How amazed David was that the majestic God would bring his care and concern down to man. For David knew that angels and men are closer to each other than either of them is to the Holy God.

The stars, the angels, the quiet hillside, the deep questions for God— it's a wonderful scene to get lost in.

The clear night sky may be one of our best pictures right now of the host of angels arrayed like stars around God's throne-room, radiating praise and worship. Go outside some night soon, and put your focus in that direction, especially if earthly concerns and difficulties are weighing you down.

Gratefully accept the Lord's invitation in Isaiah 40:26 — "Lift up your eyes and look to the heavens," and remember the one "who created all these" and who "brings out the starry host one by one, and calls them each by name."

You might recall the example of Abraham from Genesis 15. Just as you and I often do, Abraham needed something. He asked God, "O Sovereign Lord, what can you give me?" (15:2) — which is a lot like our questions of "How can you fix this problem, God?" Or, "Lord, when will you get me out of this tight spot?" Or especially, "Father, when will you do what you promised?"

In response, God took Abraham outside under a blazing night sky. He said to Abraham, "Look up at the heavens and count the stars — if indeed you can."

Maybe that's a picture of how we should think of angels. We can't count them, any more than we can count the stars. (The stronger our telescopes, the more stars there are to count!)

But like David, we can see in those stars an amazing picture of God's care and concern for us. It's a love coming through not only by way of thousands or millions of angels whom God created to serve us, but also in a thousand or a million other ways as well. His grace is "one blessing after another" (John 1:16).

Look up at the stars and be amazed. Then trust God and find his reward, as Abraham did: "Abram believed the Lord, and the Lord credited it to him as righteousness" (15:6).

So the stars are a good reminder of angels, but also of something more.

The book of Revelation opens with John's vision of the glorified Jesus Christ. John saw Jesus holding something: "In his right hand he held seven *stars*" (1:16). What are these stars? Jesus himself tells us: 'The mystery of the seven stars that you saw in my right hand . . . is this: The seven stars are the *angels* of the seven churches" (1:20).

The next few pages in Revelation give us messages from Jesus Christ to each of these "seven churches," located in seven cities in Asia Minor where Christians were established. Each message is addressed identically: "To the *angel* of the church. . . ." Who are these seven "angels," who are also pictured as seven stars?

The best explanation seems to be that they're the pastors leading and shepherding those seven churches. They're charged by the Lord Jesus with faithfully communicating his Word to the people in these seven churches. They were his messengers, his ambassadors.

In this sense, we too can be more like angels than we might have thought possible. For we, too, have been charged by the Lord Jesus with faithfully communicating his divine message — the gospel.

> God was reconciling the world to himself in Christ, not counting men's sins against them. And *he has committed to us the message of reconciliation.* We are therefore Christ's ambassadors, as though God were making his appeal through us. (2 Corinthians 5:19-20)

That's why we too can be like stars, as long as we don't let our grumbling selfishness get in the way of our testimony. Paul says it like this:

> Do everything without complaining or arguing, so that you may become blameless and pure, children of God without fault in a

crooked and depraved generation, in which *you shine like stars* in the universe as you hold out the word of life…. (Philippians 2:14-16)

If you want to be like an angel — even to the extent of shining like a star — then stop your grumbling and wrangling, and let God mold you into a faithful sharer of the Word of Life. The world out there is dark, and desperately needs your starlight.

The next time you see a night sky charged with stars, think about angels…and think about yourself.

Chapter Six

WHEN ANGELS APPEAR

THERE'S NO WAY to fathom how often angels have been involved in your life. One may be at your side right now, helping you turn the pages of this book. (What an honor that would be for both of us!)

But we can't know for sure, because angels are mostly invisible. That can seem bothersome, but Billy Graham helps us see it in perspective:

> While angels may become visible by choice, our eyes are not con-
> structed to see them ordinarily any more than we can see the dimen-
> sions of a nuclear field, the structure of atoms, or the electricity that
> flows through copper wiring. Our ability to sense reality is limited:
> The deer of the forest far surpass our human capacity in their keen-
> ness of smell. Bats possess a phenomenally sensitive built-in radar
> system. Some animals can see things in the dark that escape our
> attention. Swallows and geese possess sophisticated guidance sys-
> tems that appear to border on the supernatural. So why should we
> think it strange if men fail to perceive the evidences of angelic pres-
> ence?

Sometimes, though, angels show up in Scripture in ordinary human form. Gideon at first didn't seem to recognize the person standing before him as an angel (Judges 6:12-13). Nor did Samson's father, Manoah (Judges 13:16) — though Manoah's wife was quicker on the uptake. "A man of God came to me," she told her husband. "He looked like an angel of God, very awesome" (13:6).

When angels came to rescue Lot and his family from Sodom, Lot assumed they were only men as he greeted them, then invited them into his home and off the wretched streets of Sodom, and showered them with hospitality (Genesis 19:1-3).

Before rescuing Lot, these same heavenly beings had been calling on his famous uncle. "While he was sitting at the entrance to his tent in the heat of the day," the passage tells us, "Abraham looked up and saw three *men* standing nearby" (18:1-2). Abraham also lavished hospitality on these visitors whom he first perceived as men, and after they washed up they ate Sarah's cooking. But Abraham, the man of faith and the friend of God, seemed quicker to grasp the Lord's presence in these "men" than Lot was.

The New Testament implies that it's still possible to receive angelic visitors who appear to be only human. Remember that bit about this in Hebrews 13:2? We're told, "Do not forget to entertain strangers, for by so doing some people have entertained angels without knowing it." If you really believe in angels and would enjoy entertaining or honoring them (as a thank-you gesture perhaps for everything they do for you), consider improving your hospitality to strangers. Not until eternity will you know if any of them were angels, but the possibility anyway is exciting. (Of course, there's an even stronger motive for being gracious and giving to those you don't know well. Jesus said in Matthew 25:35, "I was a stranger and you took me in." If we respect and serve strangers, the Lord counts it as service done to *himself.*)

More frequent in Scripture than the undetected appearances of heavenly spirits are the times when there's no mistake about it: There's an angel on the scene.

Jacob was certain. He was heading home to the land of his grandfather Abraham and his father Isaac, when on the way, "the angels of God met him" (Genesis 32:1). And his response when he saw them? It was a shout: "This is the camp of God!" (32:2). Jacob still had some wrestling to do with the Lord, but his sensitivities were on the right track. He knew God was with him.

Daniel was even more certain about what he saw. His report in Daniel 10 of the awesome figure he saw on the riverbank has been called Scripture's most detailed description of an angel's appearance. Notice how much Daniel observed:

> I looked up and there before me was a man dressed in linen, with a belt of the finest gold around his waist. His body was like chrysolite [a yellow or golden stone], his face like lightning, his eyes like flaming torches his arms and legs like the gleam of burnished bronze, and his voice like the sound of a multitude. (10:5-6)

You can tell Daniel took more than a brief look, and it's no wonder the experience drained him. "I had no strength left," he says. "my face turned deathly pale and I was helpless" (10:8). The squinting alone would have given anyone a headache.

We've already seen in lots of other Scriptures how angels appear in various degrees of light and fire and glory. But it's worth another dazzling look. Notice, for example, what's recorded about the color of their clothing after Jesus had risen from the dead:

The angel who rolled back the stone from Jesus' tomb had an appearance "like lightning, and his clothes were white as snow" (Matthew 28:3). As various women came to the tomb, the angels they saw are described as "a young man dressed in a white robe" (Mark 16:5), and "two angels in white" (John 20:12) and "two men in clothes that gleamed like lightning" (Luke 24:4).

Forty days later the angels on the ground when Jesus ascended into heaven appeared to the disciples as "two men dressed in white" (Acts 1:10).

Years later, the angelic and worshipful creatures whom John saw as twenty-four elders "were dressed in white and had crowns of gold on their heads" (Revelation 4:4).

The color white in Scripture is associated not only with purity but also with joy. "Eat your food with gladness, and drink your wine with a joyful heart," we're advised in Ecclesiastes 9:7-8, "for it is now that God favors what you do. *Always be clothed in white,* and always anoint your head with oil."

The soul-stirring fulfillment of that instruction for God's people is foretold in Revelation 7. In his vision John saw a countless multitude from among all the world's ethnic groups standing before God. "They were *wearing white robes* and were holding palm branches in their hands."

The angels joined in their joyful praise to God. Then one of those elders dressed in white told John that these human worshipers "have washed their robes and made them *white* in the blood of the Lamb" (7:14).

Joy was assured for this white-robed multitude, because the elder promised John that "God will wipe away every tear from their eyes" (7:17).

The whiteness gets even more dazzling as we picture the Lord's ride to final victory with his angels. Enjoy this scene with John:

> I saw heaven standing open and there before me was *a white horse, whose rider is called Faithful and True.* With justice he judges and makes war. His eyes are like blazing fire, and on his head are many crowns. He has a name written on him that no one knows but he himself. He is dressed in a robe dipped in blood, and his name is the Word of God. The armies of heaven were following him, *riding on white horses and dressed in fine linen, white and clean.* (Revelation 19:11-14)

Pure, snow-white joy is what awaits us as we share in the pure, snow-white victory of the Lord and his angels.

Our Eyes Opened to See Them

Getting a glimpse of angels doesn't depend solely on what form God happens to give them. Scripture lends support to the fact that the Lord must open our eyes before we can see them.

Sometimes in Scripture—as in the case with Daniel and his companions on the bank of the Tigris (Daniel 10)—one person could see the angel, but the people beside him couldn't.

And one time a donkey could see the angel, but the person riding him couldn't.

That was Balaam's donkey. The greater miracle in that story isn't so much a donkey getting to *talk* about an angel, but a man like Balaam getting to *see* an angel.

Remember the story? Balaam was internationally known as a diviner—part magician, part prophet, so to speak, and the king of curses and blessings. He was a "seer"—he was supposed to "see" what others couldn't. If anybody in the world should have been expected to spot angels, it was Balaam.

One day he was invited by the King Balak of Moab to call down curses on Israel. God communicated his thoughts on that subject right away. He commanded Balaam not to return with the Moabite princes who had hand-delivered the king's invitation. He said Israel was blessed, not cursed.

That should have been the end of it for Balaam.

But the king of Moab sent his invitation again, this time by way of princes "more numerous and more distinguished than the first" (Numbers 22:15). Plus, the king upped his promised payment for Balaam's curses. "I will reward you handsomely," he said (22:17).

Balaam, therefore, said he would check things out again with God.

Fifteen centuries later, the apostle Peter would precisely define Balaam's character this way: He "loved the wages of wickedness" (2 Peter 2:15).

The Lord had a plan for accomplishing something through Balaam far bigger than this heathen diviner could comprehend. "Okay," God said that night to Balaam. "Go." A money-hungry celebrity was about to be humbled.

At sunup, Balaam was saddled and off on the road to Moab to join King Balak. Little did he know how angry God was with him.

How angry was he?

Angry enough to station his angel with drawn sword across the middle of the Moab road (and in a narrow spot at that, with no place to swerve). The poor donkey must have been as terrified as any human being ever was to see such a sight. She tried all she could to get herself and her master away from that awesome presence.

But Balaam — world-famous seer — didn't notice his visitor.

What he did notice was his donkey's strange behavior. Balaam was angry now, and he beat her with his staff. (Who's the jackass in this story anyway?)

God now performed a two-step miracle of opening what was closed. Each step was just as easy for him to do as any other miracle.

First he opened the donkey's mouth and let her speak. Balaam was enough beside himself with fury that he fell right into an argument with her. "If I had a sword in my hand," he told her, "I would kill you right now" (Numbers 22:29).

Step Two: God opened Balaam's eyes to see where a sword really was — and whose hand it was in. "He saw the angel of the Lord standing in the road with his sword drawn" (22:31).

"That donkey," the angel told him, "just saved your life."

As anybody might with a sword aimed at his neck, Balaam suddenly exhibited meekness — to all appearances anyway. God showed him amazing visions of just how blessed the people of Israel really are. Balaam remained docile long enough to pass those visions on to a very frustrated King Balak. The whole time, the image of that upraised angelic sword must have been flashing in Balaam's mind. At any moment, it just might become visible again. Balaam took no chances.

Soon, however, his fear of God wore off. What Balaam and the king of Moab couldn't do to Israel by divination, they tried to accomplish by seduction. Jesus himself uncovers their crime while speaking to John in Revelation 2:14 — "Balaam . . . taught Balak to entice the Israelites to sin by eating food sacrificed to idols and by committing sexual immorality." That sordid story is told in Numbers 25.

Balaam also got involved with the Midianites, another group of Israel's enemies, in a further attempt to seduce Israel (25:14-18). This time it cost him his life. God commanded his people to take vengeance on the Midianites. The victims' list in Numbers 31:8 is headed by the names of five Midianite kings killed by the Israelites. Then comes this entry: "They also killed Balaam son of Beor with the sword." Seeing the sword of the Lord's angel wasn't enough to reform Balaam for good. So the sword of man sent him to his eternal reckoning.

But there's a happier story in Scripture about God opening up someone's eyes to see angels. What a delight it is to hear it again.

Six hundred years after Balaam's time, Israel was at war with Syria. Elisha, the prophet of the Lord, had the power to discern all of Syria's military secrets. Naturally he would promptly share these discoveries with the king of Israel.

The Syrian king figured that kind of leak had to be fixed. He sent his forces out to capture Elisha. They located him in the town of Dothan, and surrounded the place by night with soldiers, horses, and chariots (2 Kings 6:8-14). There could be no escape.

Early the next morning Elisha's servant went out and discovered the dreadful trap. With despair he reported their predicament to his master. "What shall we do?" he cried.

Elisha told him not to fear. "Those who are with us," he said, "are more than those who are with them" (6:16).

The prophet knew that, frankly, the servant would find such optimism hard to swallow. Israel had no armies in Dothan.

So Elisha prayed: "O Lord, open his eyes so he may see."

God answered his prayer. "The Lord opened the servant's eyes, and he looked and saw the hills full of horses and chariots of fire all around" (6:17). That was *God's* army in them thar hills—his host of angels.

In the rest of the passage, the servant isn't mentioned anymore. He must have mostly been staring in wonder at what happened next. As it turned out, the sight of those angel warriors might have been only to instill brave confidence in Elisha and his companion. The angels never entered the battle. As the Syrian soldiers closed in on him, Elisha prayed for God to blind their eyes. In this condition Elisha led the Syrian troops down the road ten miles to Samaria, and into the hands of Israel's king and army. Not until then did Elisha pray for the Syrians' eyes to open. Then they discovered that instead of having Elisha for a prisoner, they were prisoners themselves. The glory for the victory was God's.

Seeing those angels must have persuaded Elisha that the strength of an enemy army is never an actual threat when you're on God's side. When Israel's king asked if he should kill the Syrian captives, Elisha said no. "Feed them instead, and send them home." The king followed Elisha's advice. The Syrians were guests at Israel's feast, then they returned to Syria. And for a time at least their warfare with Israel ended.

A modern yet similar story is told by Doug Connelly in his book *Angels Around Us*. In the early 1950s, a missionary group in Kenya learned of an imminent attack on their mission by Mau Mau warriors. To defend their families as well as they could, the men put up a barbed wire barricade and turned on the few floodlights. With what few weapons they had they stood guard along the mission's perimeter, while their wives and children prayed inside.

They waited. But no attack came.

Months later a converted Mau Mau tribesman explained that just as he and his fellow warriors prepared to attack the mission from all sides, large fiery figures appeared from out of the night. They stood between the Mau Mau and the missionaries, racing in a circle around the barricade. Frightened by the sight of these creatures, the Mau Mau fled.

"The missionaries may not have seen them," Connelly writes, "but God opened the warriors' eyes to what normally would have been invisible — His band of holy angels."

Sometimes when angels intervene on the fields of human conflict, God opens the eyes of both sides to see his heavenly beings at work. In her book *Angels,* Hope Price records two hopeless situations in World War I related by a British captain. The first occurred early in the war near Mons, France, where outnumbered British troops had been fighting for days without relief.

> They had lost many men and guns, and defeat looked inevitable. Captain Cecil W Hayward was there and tells how suddenly, in the midst of a gun battle, firing on both sides stopped. To their astonishment, the British troops saw "four or five wonderful beings, much bigger than men," between themselves and the Germans. These "men" were bare-headed, wore white robes and seemed to float rather than stand. Their backs were to the British and their arms and hands were outstretched toward the Germans.
>
> At that moment, the horses ridden by German cavalrymen became terrified and stampeded off in every direction.
>
> Hayward also told of another battle sometime later in World War I when matters again seemed hopeless for British soldiers, who were surrounded by German troops. Suddenly the heavy enemy fire stopped completely, and everything grew strangely quiet.
>
> Then "the sky opened with a bright shining light, and figures of luminous beings appeared floating between the British and German lines."

German troops retreated in disorder, allowing the Allied forces to reform and fall back on a line of defense farther to the west.

German prisoners were taken that day, and when they were asked why they surrendered when they had the British troops surrounded, they looked amazed, saying, "But there were hosts and hosts of you!"

Hope Price comments in her book that the British government officially sponsored national days of prayer during the conflict. She believes the government's commitment to prayer played a role in the angelic intervention on behalf of the British soldiers.

No doubt the key event in the missionaries' story from Kenya during the Mau Mau uprisings was the praying being done inside the mission by the women and children. Many a godly teacher has reminded us over the centuries that all that the Lord does on our behalf is in answer to someone's prayer. That surely includes sending angels to our rescue, plus opening our eyes to see them.

There must be quite a lot of intervening angels around that we just never notice — but sometimes, when the time is right, God takes the scales off our eyes so we can see them.

Appearing in Dreams

Before moving on from angels' visibility, remember too that angels can show themselves in our dreams. Jacob saw angels that way at two crucial times in his life. He saw them first on a stairway to heaven when he was alone and camping out while running away from home (Genesis 28). Many years later they appeared in a dream in which God told him it was time to go back (31:10-13).

The New Testament story of Joseph the husband of Mary contains the most dream appearances by angels in the Scriptures. It also contains some of the strongest examples of obedience. Joseph didn't get into angelmania

WHEN ANGELS APPEAR 101

from all of his supernatural experiences. He just did what God's angel told him to do.

While we study his story, let's ask ourselves these questions: *How is my own track record in obedience? Is it strong enough that God could trust me to obey his special instructions delivered through an angel in a dream?*

Notice what thorough and specific directions Joseph receives on the first night an angel comes to him.

> An *angel* of the Lord appeared to him *in a dream* and said, "Joseph son of David, do not be afraid to take Mary home as your wife, because what is conceived in her is from the Holy Spirit. She will give birth to a son, and you are to give him the name Jesus, because he will save his people from their sins." (Matthew 1:20-21)

Joseph gets the what and the how and the why. Now see for yourself how thorough Joseph is in his response.

> When Joseph woke up, he did what the angel of the Lord had commanded him and took Mary home as his wife. But he had no union with her until she gave birth to a son. And he gave him the name Jesus. (1:24-25)

Joseph has proven himself. God has his man, and he can use the same, intimate channel again to communicate to him. Look closely at the next directions Joseph obtains by night courier, this time after the wise men had left Bethlehem:

> An *angel* of the Lord appeared to Joseph *in a dream*. "Get up," he said, "take the child and his mother and escape to Egypt. Stay there until I tell you, for Herod is going to search for the child to kill him." (2:13)

Again, judge his response, and notice how Joseph fulfills prophetic Scripture by simply obeying God.

So he got up, took the child and his mother during the night and left for Egypt, where he stayed until the death of Herod. And so was fulfilled what the Lord had said through the prophet: "Out of Egypt I called my son." (2:14-15)

Watch the process a third time...

After Herod died, an *angel* of the Lord appeared *in a dream* to Joseph in Egypt and said, "Get up, take the child and his mother and go to the land of Israel, for those who were trying to take the child's life are dead."

So he got up, took the child and his mother and went to the land of Israel. (2:19-21)

And a fourth, with prophetic fulfillment again:

But when he heard that Archelaus was reigning in Judea in place of his father Herod, he was afraid to go there. Having been warned *in a dream*, he withdrew to the district of Galilee, and he went and lived in a town called Nazareth. So was fulfilled what was said through the prophets: "He will be called a Nazarene." (2:22-23)

In this last situation, an angel isn't mentioned as being in the dream. If an angel did appear to Joseph, obviously it isn't important enough to be recorded. What was important for Joseph is what's also crucial for all of us: We're to obey, whether or not God's instruction comes through an angel.

The Sound of Angels

Learning about angels and dreams helps us see that these heavenly beings can access us through senses other than sight.

Sometimes it may be only the *sound* of angels that human beings can perceive. It was that way once for David and his fighting men (2 Samuel 5:22-25). With the enemy Philistines spread out before him in a valley,

David asked God what to do. God told him not to try a direct attack, but instead to have his men circle behind the enemy, to a place where balsam trees were growing.

And there, the Lord told David, they should listen for the sound of angel warriors.

> As soon as you hear *the sound of marching in the tops of the balsam trees,* move quickly, because that will mean the Lord has gone out in front of you to strike the Philistine army.

Men don't march in treetops, but angels can. David did what the Lord told him, and the result was another in Israel's string of victories through David's obedience to God.

Angels definitely know how to make noise. The angel in Revelation 10:3 "gave a loud shout like the roar of a lion. When he shouted, the voices of the seven thunders spoke." Seven thunders is no whisper.

In Isaiah's vision, the seraphs are calling to one another, "Holy, holy, holy is the Lord Almighty." But they weren't just murmuring a phrase or humming their way through a hymn. "At the sound of their voices," Isaiah says, "the doorposts and thresholds shook." That's real vibes.

"Strange," says H. A. Ironside on this verse, "that inanimate pillars should thus be moved while the hearts of men remain obdurate and motionless!" Amen.

Angels apparently have their own spiritual languages, though 1 Corinthians 13 makes it clear that these "tongues of angels" are not as important or as beautiful in God's eyes as the simple human language of our love in action.

Do angels sing? Usually we assume that they do, and many a Christmas pageant includes a musical number from an angel choir.

Surprisingly, however, the Scriptures don't clearly indicate the angels singing as often as you might think. In a passage such as the Christmas story in Luke 2, some English versions and paraphrases say that the angels were "singing" their praises of "Glory to God in the highest," but the Greek word simply means that they were "saying" these words. The same is true of the word sometimes translated "singing" in Revelation 5:13, where "every creature in heaven and on earth and under the earth and on the sea" joins in an exalted expression of praise to God and to the Lamb.

A stronger reference to angel song might be a passage we looked at earlier — Job 38:7, where "the morning stars *sang* together and all the angels shouted for joy." The Hebrew word translated here as "sang" is usually used in reference to singing.

But mostly in the Bible when it comes to singing, it's God's people who make the music, not angels.

My friend and great preacher W. A. Criswell explored an interesting reason for this, one that reminds us of Paul's words in Romans 8:22 that "the whole creation has been groaning…right up to the present time":

> Music is made up of major chords and minor chords. The minor chords speak of the wretchedness, death and sorrow of this fallen creation. Most of nature moans and groans in a plaintive and minor key. The sound of the wind through the forest, the sound of the storm, the sound of the wind around the house, is always in a minor key. It wails. The sound of the ocean moans in its restlessness, in its speechless trouble. Even the nightingale's song, the sweetest song of the birds, is the saddest. Most of the sounds of nature are in a minor key. It reflects the wretchedness, the despair, the hurt, the agony, the travail of this fallen creation.
>
> But the angel knows nothing of it. An angel knows nothing of wretchedness, nothing of despair, nothing of the fall of our lost race….
>
> Our sweetest songs with deepest sorrows are fraught. Somehow it is the sorrow of life, the disappointment of life and the despair of life that makes people sing, either in the blackness of its hour or in the

glory of its deliverance. That is why the redeemed sing and angels just speak of it. They see it, they watch it, but they know nothing about it. For it takes a lost and fallen man — who has been brought back to God, who has been forgiven of his sin, who has been redeemed — it takes a saved soul to sing!

Yet it's fine to believe that angels can and do sing, because just as Scripture doesn't pointedly show them singing their praises, neither does it insist that they *can't*. Billy Graham says the idea of angels never singing "seems inconceivable." He reminds us that angels certainly "possess the ultimate capacity to offer praise," and that music has always been a universal language for praise. He also points to the testimony of dying believers who said they "heard the music of heaven."

He concludes: "I believe that angels have the capacity to employ heavenly celestial music." He suggests that "in heaven we will be taught the language and music of the celestial world." But he also notes that

> before we can understand the music of heaven we will have to go beyond our earthly concept of music. I think most earthly music will seem to us to have been in the "minor key" in comparison to what we are going to hear in heaven.

The question of angels singing is linked to our own nature and destiny as human beings. It's time to look closer at that now — to understand better how angels are like us, and how they're different.

Chapter Seven

THE ANGELS AND US: HOW MUCH ALIKE?

W E'VE SEEN ENOUGH by now to know God's angels differ from you and me in many remarkable ways. But one distinction towers above all others. It's a desperate difference, a contrast that has rocked the course of universal history. We have to understand this profound difference before we can fully appreciate the ways in which we and angels are alike — and how we'll be alike in the future.

That difference is this: God's good angels are still what they were created to be; you and I are not.

Ever since the flaming sword of the cherubim flashed across Eden's gate, the life God created for our enjoyment has been out of our reach. All human flesh has fallen short of the Lord's intended purpose for mankind. Sin infected us all, enslaved us all, and cursed us all with death and the fear of it. You and I were ruined. As Adam and Eve's children we were conceived in sin and born only to die. As we grew, each of us only confirmed our condemnation by selfish, destructive choices.

Throughout human history no father's son and no mother's daughter was born outside this predicament. Humanly speaking there was no escape, no hope for a cure. You and I were utterly doomed.

But then—*God* sent his Son to be born into human flesh and to take upon *himself* all the curse and the death and the doom that was ours. Then with power he proved his total victory over all of it by rising from the dead.

When by faith you and I grasp what really happened here, we too rise up from our chains. We stand amazed and forever grateful and filled with unspeakable joy.

And what do the angels think about all this?

The apostle Peter tells us they are gripped with an abiding curiosity about it. And I suppose they always will be.

Our Salvation Makes Them Curious

After Peter warms our hearts in 1 Peter 1 with a description of our salvation, he adds, "Even angels long to look into these things" (1:12). What exactly are "these things"? Don't angels already understand the details of our salvation better than we do? Surely they have a better vantage point than we do down here.

Peter's words are a good reminder that what counts in the Christian life is personal experience, not head knowledge. Yes, angels certainly have intellectual awareness—"head knowledge"—of our salvation. But they haven't *felt* salvation or feasted on it. Therefore they "long to look into these things" because they understand that personal acquaintance is far better than mental comprehension. They have no pride about what they merely know; they long instead for *experience*.

Just look back over the first eleven verses of 1 Peter 1. See how much of it must be outside what angels can personally encounter.

As people chosen for salvation in Christ we have been "sprinkled by his blood" (1:2). Angels have never known this cleansing that's available to us constantly.

We've been given "new birth" (1:3). Angels can never know the freshness of being born again.

This new birth comes our way through God's "great mercy" (1:3). Angels have never needed his mercy because they've never sinned.

God promises us a rich and indestructible inheritance that's being "kept in heaven for you" (1:4). Angels already have what's theirs. As far as we know there's nothing for them to inherit. The riches they see stacked and stored in heaven are for us.

We have "a living hope" (1:3). Our hope is that our faith will "result in praise, glory and honor when Jesus Christ is revealed" (1:7). The angels have no need of hope since Christ's glory is already a present reality to them.

Peter tells us this about Jesus: "Though you have not seen him, you love him" (1:8). The angels *do* see Jesus, and surely they love him too. But tell me: Which do you think is more precious — true love from those who already see the Lord, or true love from those who still must wait to get their first glimpse of his glorious face?

Peter drives deeper. He tells us, "Even though you do not see him now, you *believe* in him" (1:8). We believe. We have no choice but to walk by faith because the Lord is not within our sight. But angels have no need of belief. They know the Lord by sight, not by faith.

Because of our faith, Peter says, we're "filled with an inexpressible and glorious joy" (1:8). It seems obvious in Scripture that angels know plenty about "glorious joy." But which would you say is more wonderful — the rejoicing of those who stay by God's throne, or the rejoicing by faith of those who can only imagine what heaven is like?

Peter tells us more. During this "little while" that we live on earth we must endure "all kinds of trials," and these trials cause us to "suffer grief" (1:6). As far as we know, angels lose no loved ones, nor experience lingering trials of personal grief and loss.

All our own sufferings, however, have a greater purpose, one that allows us to be thankful for them:

These have come *so that your faith* — of greater worth than gold, which perishes even though refined by fire — *may be proved genuine....* (1:7)

Proven, genuine faith in God is what you and I really want, isn't it? Right now we long for the day when we can shout, "See, it really is true! I was right to believe! I was right to take God at his word!" We know that day is coming. So right now we rejoice — "for we are receiving the goal of our faith, the salvation of our souls" (1:9).

No wonder Peter adds the line about the angels wanting to explore this salvation inside-out. When he says that "even angels long to look into these things," the single Greek word translated as "to look into" is a term with intensity. It pictures someone "stooping over to look." This is not a quick glimpse, but a calculated, close-up analysis — a deliberate gaze, a studied observation. That's what angels wish they could do with our salvation.

In the Gospels this same verb is used three times for someone actually bending over to look inside Jesus' empty tomb on that first Easter Sunday morning: Peter himself (in Luke 24:12), the apostle John (John 20:5), and Mary Magdalene (John 20:11). You can easily imagine with what intense curiosity all three of them stared at the place where they fully expected the dead body of their Lord to be, but where now they plainly saw it was not.

Maybe that's a hint of another picture: Today the angels wish they could bend over and look inside what was once as empty and cold as a tomb — our spirits — and see and feel and experience just how the living Christ can be there inside us through his Holy Spirit.

Angels can only long to experience this — but we already can!

Thank God he had the answer for our enslavement — a cure for the curse and the doom. That answer is my salvation through Christ. But the joy of it can be fully known only because of the despair that came first.

Until I discovered last year I had cancer, I never seriously doubted I would live out a full life on this earth. Then, after I had looked death in the face, being told that my disease was in remission was the greatest news I could imagine. Being saved is like that too. If we didn't know the hopelessness of being lost we could never appreciate the hope of being saved.

I remember what it was like to go to bed at night and worry about what would happen to me if I woke up somewhere other than that room where I'd gone to sleep. Then one day I trusted Jesus as my Savior, and knew my sin was forgiven. That worry went away.

To their benefit, angels have never known such worry or any depression or despair. But they've also never known the stunning power of the hope that can come after the hopelessness. Since they can't say, "I know what it's like to be lost," they also can't say, "I know what it's like to be found." They can't imagine being overwhelmed with a burden of failure and guilt, then one day to be overwhelmed with joy as the Holy Spirit ignites the discovery in our heart that Jesus has come and forgiven it all.

A great hymn I heard often in my childhood comes to mind here. I remember our singing "Holy, Holy, Is What the Angels Sing" in special services and evangelistic crusades in the church my father pastored. It was written in 1924 by Rev. Johnson Oatman Jr. and John R. Sweeney, and the chorus goes,

> Holy, Holy, is what the angels sing.
> And I expect to help them make the courts of heaven ring.
> But when I sing redemption's story, they will fold their wings,
> for angels never felt the joy that our salvation brings.

As great and mighty as angels are, they can only guess at the joy of a single moment when the Lord Jesus wipes a tear from our eye and the stain from our heart.

It kind of feels good to be one up on the angels, doesn't it? Isn't it wonderful to be redeemed! Isn't it wonderful to be forgiven!

So that's a strong explanation for why angels long to explore the hope of our salvation. But there's another reason that may be even stronger.

Our Salvation Makes Them Rejoice

When we see what angels possess in power and light and constant closeness to God, it's easy to envy them. We're tempted to prefer an angel's existence to our own. It makes us wonder which would be better: to be sinless and never need salvation, or to be a sinner who's found the joy of being saved and forgiven?

I suppose there's been more than one discussion about that through the years. We could debate it for eternity. But it wouldn't make any difference. I was born into a fallen race as a lost human being, and trying to assume what it would be like to never have sinned is ridiculous. I don't even have the option.

Angels, likewise, can't fully imagine what's it's like to be in my condition. Redemption for them is not a personal reality to enjoy. But they can be excited about it on *my* behalf.

Jesus says, "There is rejoicing *in the presence of the angels of God* over one sinner who repents" (Luke 15:10). It sets off a party in heaven whenever someone on earth recognizes his need for the Savior and responds correctly.

Revelation 5:9-14 provides an awesome picture of angelic joy over our salvation, and points clearly to what may be the deepest reason for their elation. In this passage the "twenty-four elders" praise Christ for being worthy to open the scroll and break its seven seals, something no one else could do. *"You were slain,"* these angelic beings cry out to Christ, *"and with your blood* you purchased men for God from every tribe and language and people and nation."

Suddenly their worship is joined by "the voice of many angels, numbering thousands upon thousands, and ten thousand times ten thousand." This massive angel choir offers up its praise "in a loud voice":

> Worthy is the Lamb, who was slain,
>> to receive power and wealth and wisdom and strength
>> and honor and glory and praise!

Here in the high places which have always been their home, the angels' praise centers on this: the entrance into God's holy heaven of those who don't deserve to be there, *all through the blood of the murdered Son of God.*

This sacrifice of Christ must bring angels the most astonishment of all. How in the vastness of eternity could the Lord of Heaven's Armies ever be killed? How in all divine infinity could there be reason enough for God to take on human flesh and blood in the first place, let alone to have it pierced and spilled, and surrendered to death at the hands of wicked rebels?

I can imagine the angels thinking, "If the redemption and rescue of human beings is worth *that much* to the Lord — if it's worth the pure and precious life-blood of the eternal Son of God — then this salvation demands our eternal attention and our unceasing contemplation."

And think about this: Angels are able to rejoice over what they do not fully understand and experience. What an example for us! If they rejoice over a salvation they don't even get to share in and can't even fully understand — how much more should we, the saved ones, live in constant joy!

It's true of course that there are many deep wells in the Christian life we haven't yet dipped into, and many deep mysteries we haven't understood. But can't we go ahead with joy and offer God the worship he deserves for all his riches, even if we haven't embraced them all ourselves?

That's something we can learn from angels.

And now that we've got a good grasp of the big differences between human beings and angels, let's look more at how we're alike.

Angels Are God's Servants (And So Are We)

Scripture directly mentions at least three ways in which we're like angels. Together they point especially to our eternal future, which we'll enjoy in the angels' presence.

When the apostle John wanted to worship an angel, the point the angel made in his reply (after telling John, "No, don't do it!") was how alike he and John were. It happened both times. First:

But he said to me, "…I am a *fellow servant with you* and with your brothers who hold to the testimony of Jesus." (Revelation 19:10)

And then:

But he said to me, "…I am a *fellow servant with you* and with your brothers the prophets and of all who keep the words of this book." (22:9)

The angel was God's servant, just as John and the prophets were God's servants, and just as all of us are God's servants when we speak a word of testimony for his sake and on his behalf.

Servant is one of the most commonly used names in Scripture for those who follow the Lord — and especially those whom we might more readily call "leaders." The apostles didn't deck themselves out with lofty titles. Their favorite term to describe themselves was simply God's "servants." Paul, Peter, James, Jude, and John himself all used it (just check out the opening verse in Romans, 2 Peter, James, Jude, and Revelation).

Likewise in the Old Testament, Moses, Joshua, Samuel, David, and Elijah are all called God's servants (Exodus 14:31, Joshua 24:29, 1 Samuel 3:10, 2 Samuel 3:18, 2 Kings 9:36).

The "higher" you go in God's family the more you're called upon to serve. Even if somehow you reached the equivalent of angel status in this life, you would still be simply a servant doing your duty to God. Angels, too, are servants — "ministering spirits sent to serve."

Paul once complimented the Galatians for treating him like an angel: "You welcomed me as if I were an angel of God," he said, and "as if I were Christ Jesus himself" (4:14). The Galatians probably didn't fall down in fearful awe and worship at Paul's presence; more likely they simply showed him heartfelt gratitude and respect for his service to them, which was just as the angels and Christ himself had served them.

But service isn't for leaders and angels only. "Serve one another in love," Paul says to all of us. When we reach heaven we all want to hear the commendation, "Well done, good and faithful servant!" from the Lord's lips. So we serve others now as we serve God, since that's the example Jesus set for us. "Whoever serves me must follow me," he tells us, "and where I am, my servant also will be" (John 12:26).

Our privilege of being able to offer service to God will continue in eternity. John saw my future and yours in his vision: Those who've been washed in the Lamb's blood "are before the throne of God and serve him day and night in his temple" (Revelation 7:15). When the new Jerusalem comes, "The throne of God and of the Lamb will be in the city, and *his servants will serve him*" (22:3).

Let's grow in learning and loving to serve him now, that we may all the more enjoy serving him then.

Angels Are Immortal (And So Are We)

Jesus mentions two other ways in which we will be like the angels in eternity.

First, we'll no longer experience marriage as we do now. Jesus said, "When the dead rise, they will neither marry nor be given in marriage; they will be like the angels in heaven" (Mark 12:25). The gladness and fulfillment we will know in our perfect, heavenly union with Christ will transcend any satisfaction we've known in marriage. Human marriage, after all, is a temporary picture reflecting an eternal reality — which is Christ's relationship with his bride, the Church (Ephesians 5:25-32). Our joy in the future reality will far exceed our pleasure in the present scenario.

The second way we'll be like angels is that we can then no longer experience death. Jesus says in Luke 20:36 that those who are raised to eternity "can no longer die; for they are like the angels." As spiritual beings, angels know nothing of what it's like to get ill, grow old, and eventually die. Someday we, too, will be beyond the reach of those afflictions.

God's angels are known as the "elect" angels (1 Timothy 5:21), indicating that God chose to let them live eternally in his heaven. Christians are also are called "the elect" (2 Timothy 2:10). The angels themselves will be sent by God to "gather his elect from the four winds" (Matthew 24:31), for we too are chosen for eternal life. We and the angels will share permanent citizenship in God's heavenly kingdom forever.

The difference is in how and why we get to stay there. C. F. Dickason explains that angels were elected "unto perseverance," while Christians have been elected "unto redemption." He says the good angels who did not fall in Satan's rebellion "remain fixed in holiness." They are incapable of sin, just as we will be in eternity. But we will be there in heaven only because the blood of Christ has washed away our sins. The "perseverance" and "fixed holiness" that God provides the angels helps assure us that in heaven we also will be truly free from "this body of sin" (Romans 6:6).

Like us, angels are not eternal from of old, as Christ is. Their immortality is like ours: They are merely created beings who were given eternal life in heaven by God (and never lost it). Even in eternity, in the presence of the eternal God, neither we nor the angels will ever be on God's level. M. J. Erickson explains this from the human point of view:

> Even when redeemed and glorified, we will still be renewed human beings. We will never become God. He will always be God and we will always be humans.... Salvation consists in God's restoring us to what he intended us to be, not elevating us to what he is.

It's the same conclusion from the angels' perspective. Angels are always just angels, while God will always be God.

Since angels never die, the ones we see in heaven will be the same angels we read about in the Bible. Won't it be thrilling to meet Gabriel and Michael, and the angel who locked the lions' jaws for Daniel, and the one who set aside the stone from Jesus' tomb, and the one who sprang Peter out of jail, and all the others?

But even today, just think: Those same angels are carrying on their invisible ministry to us right now.

Angels Have Personality (And So Do We)

Since Jesus indicates that our heavenly existence will be like that of the angels in some essential ways, this could well be our signal to consider other similarities also.

The most logical assumption along this line is that as spiritual beings we'll continue to have personality, just as the angels do. In fact we'll doubtless have a much stronger and more fulfilled sense of personhood than we have now. We should never fear that in heaven we'll turn into wispy wallflowers with little to say or do. That certainly doesn't describe the angels.

Have you picked up just how powerful their personalities are? Listen to some snatches of angel speech, and ask yourself: Do these sound like slow drifters talking, or like strong, action-oriented personalities with intelligence and purpose? What do their words tell you about their mental and communication abilities?

> "Look with your eyes and hear with your ears and pay attention to everything I am going to show you, for that is why you have been brought here."

> "I have now come to give you insight and understanding."

> "I have come to explain to you what will happen to your people in the future, for the vision concerns a time yet to come."

> "I will tell you what is written in the Book of Truth."

> "There will be a time of distress such as has not happened from the beginning of nations until then.... Multitudes who sleep in the dust of the earth will awake: some to everlasting life, others to shame and everlasting contempt."

"We have gone throughout the earth and found the whole world at rest and in peace."

"Your wife...will bear you a son.... He will go on before the Lord... to turn the hearts of the fathers to their children and the disobedient to the wisdom of the righteous — to make ready a people prepared for the Lord."

"I am Gabriel. I stand in the presence of God, and I have been sent to speak to you and to tell you this good news. And now you will be silent and not able to speak."

"Do not be afraid. I bring you good news of great joy that will be for all the people."

"Why do you look for the living among the dead? He is not here; he has risen!"

"There will be no more delay!... The mystery of God will be accomplished."

"The kingdom of the world has become the kingdom of our Lord and of his Christ, and he will reign for ever and ever." *(Ezekiel 40:4, Daniel 9:22, 10:14, 10:21, 12:1-2; Zechariah 1:11, Luke 1:13-17, 1:19, 2:10, 24:5-6, Revelation 10:6-7, 11:15)*

These angels certainly have their wits about them. They don't just have personality — they've got *class* and *style*, even while they're being so direct and businesslike. I'm guessing that in heaven, you and I will be something like them.

Already Up There with Them

Yes, it will be thrilling to be around these fellows all the time.

But there's a sense in which we're already in the presence of angels. I'm referring not to the fact that they're "here" watching over us, but rather that we're already "up there" with them.

Wait a minute, you're thinking. *Has this author got his head in the clouds?* Perhaps, but maybe that isn't so bad. Look with me at these profound verses.

Paul says in Ephesians 1:3 that God "has blessed us in *the heavenly realms* with every spiritual blessing in Christ." He's not speaking in future tense here. He doesn't say God *"will"* give us these blessings, but that he *"has* blessed us." He's already blessed us *in heaven.*

Notice how this picture gets even clearer in the next chapter:

> And God raised us up with Christ and seated us with him in the heavenly realms in Christ Jesus. (2:6)

Paul speaks in terms of what's already happened. We've already been raised up with Christ and placed with him (and *in* him) in the heavenly realms. There's a real sense in which we're in heaven already.

I know what you're thinking: Maybe we're already in heaven in some symbolic or mystical way, some imagined way that removes the distinction between future and present and past. But let's face it: Our feet are very much planted on solid earth. Tomorrow morning we've got tough hills to climb, tough bills to pay, and tough pills to swallow. That's reality, and it isn't heaven by a long shot.

But Paul won't let us off so easily. He tells us to deliberately fix our focus on those "blessings in Christ" up there:

> Since, then, you have been raised with Christ, *set your hearts on things above,* where Christ is seated at the right hand of God. *Set your minds on things above, not on earthly things.* (Colossians 3:1-2)

"Things above" must surely include angels, since they're such a fixture in the heavenly landscape. Our *hearts* are to be set in that direction, and so are our *minds*. That doesn't leave much of us to get engrossed in matters here on earth, does it?

Why does Paul gives us such impractical instructions? I think it's because he knows there's only one who can truly meet our every need down here, and it's the One who's worshiped day and night by angels. Our marriages, our children, our friends, our careers, our hobbies, our weekends, our retirement — none of that will meet those deepest needs that are such a reality in our life. Only Christ can meet them, and his reality is a place at the throne of his Father, where he prays for us and prepares a home for us in the sight of angels.

Paul knows what aching disappointment we'll experience if our affections aren't up there with Christ. I have the greatest wife a man could have, and a wonderful family, and a great job most of the time, and so many other gifts from God. But there's no way I could honestly say that these meet every need of my life.

I think that's why Paul wants us to make sure we're looking into heaven for fulfillment. And the harder the struggle down here, and the older you get, the more your heart begins to think about what it's like up there.

The man who wrote Hebrews left us some amazing words to help us visualize a heavenly focus. Near the end of his letter he says,

> You have come [not "you *will* come" — we're there already] to Mount Zion, to the heavenly Jerusalem, the city of the living God. You have come to *thousands upon thousands of angels* in joyful assembly.... (12:22)

That's part of the eternal picture we're to look at *now.* Not only have we come "to God, the judge of all men" (12:23) and "to Jesus the mediator of a new covenant, and to the sprinkled blood that speaks a better word than the blood of Abel" (12:24) — but we've also come to all those happy angels.

In our heart of hearts, in our deepest thoughts, we can be there — now.

The Angels Observe Us

For thinking that way, it may help us to realize what the angels up there are looking at, besides God.

The apostle Paul mentions how the apostles were on display "as a spectacle to the whole universe, *to angels* as well as to men" (1 Corinthians 4:9). Later he gave solemn instructions to his helper Timothy *"in the sight* of God and Christ Jesus *and the elect angels"* (1 Timothy 5:21).

Paul was certain he was in the angels' line of sight, and it seemed to really *matter* to Paul that the angels were watching him. Should we assume they're watching us too? And should it be just as important to us?

Paul seems to think we should. When he tells us to be orderly in our worship, for example, one reason he gives is simply, "because of the angels" (1 Corinthians 11:10). They themselves are the worship champions, and they're quite involved in watching how we do it. (You might remember that next Sunday morning.)

Paul touches on angel observation to a more staggering degree in Ephesians 3:10. In this letter Paul hits on high and lofty themes that strain our understanding. In chapter three Paul says God was now shedding light on a "mystery" which he had kept hidden "for ages past." This mystery had to do with the birth of the Church, which now included both Jew and Gentile in the composition of God's holy people. Why did God follow this strategy of suddenly revealing what he had earlier kept hidden?

J. B. Phillips translates Paul's answer this way:

> The purpose is that *all the angelic powers* should now see the complex wisdom of God's plan being worked out through the Church,

in conformity to that timeless purpose which he centered in Christ Jesus our Lord.

God is showing something to the angels! And that something is his wisdom on display in the Church — in us! We are the stage where God's new production is performed before a heavenly audience. We are the showroom where his latest masterpiece is unveiled to angelic applause. We are the arena where his matchless feats of skill are exhibited to the sound of angel cheers.

All this had been screened from the angels before, but not anymore. God wants the angels to see his wisdom at work in a miraculous new way —through the gospel.

They were already peering through heaven's windows when Jesus walked among us. When Paul once listed the wonders of Christ to Timothy, he included the fact that Jesus "was seen *by angels*" (1 Timothy 3:16). Jesus, too, was under their observation. They had their eyes glued on the Word who became flesh. "Beyond all question," Paul concluded, "the mystery…is great."

Paul sensed the angels watching everything about us. And they'll still be watching in the very end. Jesus lets us know that in Luke 12:8-9, as he speaks of the judgment day:

> I tell you, whoever acknowledges me before men, the Son of Man will also acknowledge him *before the angels of God.* But he who disowns me before men will be disowned *before the angels of God.*

When that day comes, what do you want the audience of angels to see and hear about *you?*

Maybe it's time to pray about it. In Revelation 5:8 we see the angels holding "golden bowls full of incense, which are the prayers of the saints." What precious prayers from you have gone up today to help fill those bowls as they rest in the holy hands of angels? Have you prayed today for God's kingdom to come? Have you prayed for his kingdom to be born in the lives of your family and friends and neighbors whom you love, but who are not yet believers? Have you prayed for his will to be done in your life, just as it's already done by the angels in heaven? Have you asked him to show you his specific will for your life today?

Later in Revelation we see an angel standing at God's altar with a golden censer. What an honored privilege this angel received:

> He was given much incense to offer, *with the prayers of all the saints*, on the golden altar before the throne. The smoke of the incense, together with the prayers of the saints, went up before God from the angel's hand. (8:3-4)

What fragrant prayers from you today will be offered on that altar, to rise up in sacred smoke to the God of the angels?

Chapter Eight

ANGELS YOU'VE HEARD ABOUT (AND MORE)

ANGELS GO by lots of names. Even before you picked up this book you'd probably heard of *cherubim* (or cherubs—but "cherubim" seems to fit these awesome creatures better) as well as *seraphim*. As far as individual angels go, you can easily recall the two most famous: Gabriel and the archangel Michael.

What else is good to know about angel groups or individuals and the names Scripture gives them?

Names mean more in the Bible—and meant more in Bible-time cultures—than they usually mean today. We grow in appreciating that when we look long and hard at what these heavenly beings are called in addition to "angels" (which, you'll remember, means "messengers").

Thrones, Powers, Rulers, Authorities

Some of the Scripture names for angels suggest that they're organized in an orderly way. Angels don't just go about their business at their own whim, and independently of one another. You'd think that if any group of beings could rightly do their own thing their own way, angels could. But apparently God carefully organizes them so they can best carry out his will. (And if that's true for the angels, do you think it's true for us too?)

Our evidence for angel organization includes a handful of terms in the New Testament referring to someone or something as "thrones," "dominions," "powers," "rulers," and "authorities." This terminology seems to imply different groupings or levels of angelic beings. Let's see what we discover as we scan some passages containing these terms.

Sometimes the references seem to be only to evil angelic forces—to Satan and his demons:

> The end will come, when [Christ] hands over the kingdom to God the Father after he has destroyed all *dominion, authority* and *power.* (1 Corinthians 15:24)

> Our struggle is not against flesh and blood, but against the *rulers,* against the *authorities,* against the *powers* of this dark world and against the spiritual forces of evil in the heavenly realms. (Ephesians 6:12)

> And having disarmed the *powers* and *authorities,* [God] made a public spectacle of them, triumphing over them by the cross. (Colossians 2:15)

Other references might have only God's good angels in view:

> [God] raised him from the dead and seated him at his right hand in the heavenly realms, far above all *rule* and *authority, power* and *dominion,* and every title that can be given, not only in the present age but also in the one to come. (Ephesians 1:20-21)

> His intent was that now, through the church, the manifold wisdom of God should be made known to the *rulers* and *authorities* in the heavenly realms…. (Ephesians 3:10)

Still other references could easily be to both good and evil beings, though in the larger picture the meaning could ultimately apply differently to God's angels than to demons:

For by [Christ] all things were created things in heaven and on earth, visible and invisible, whether *thrones* or *powers* or *rulers* or *authorities*; all things were created by him and for him. (Colossians 1:16)

You have been given fullness in Christ, who is the head over every *power* and *authority*. (Colossians 2:10)

We see one of these terms again in Romans 8:38-39, though here Paul seems to be actually distinguishing angels from "powers."

For I am convinced that neither death nor life, neither *angels* nor demons, neither the present nor the future, nor any *powers*, neither height nor depth, nor anything else in all creation, will be able to separate us from the love of God that is in Christ Jesus our Lord.

On the other hand, "powers" in this passage might simply be a broader designation that encompasses both angels and demons as well as perhaps the time forces of present and future. (We're definitely feeling our way through the mist of mystery here!)

The most important point to make about these passages is that they all proclaim the vast superiority of Christ in relation to these angelic "powers." Paul seems to bring up these terms only to show how much greater Christ is than anyone or anything else. Paul's focus here certainly does *not* seem to be on providing a complete picture of angel hierarchy.

So a timely word of caution: It's possible to get carried away in imagining the details of angelic organization.

Some theologians in centuries past delighted in working out elaborate systems of angelic groupings. One popular arrangement in the Middle Ages was a ranking of nine different levels of angels.

Thomas Aquinas, the great thirteenth-century theologian, laid hold of this traditional nine orders of angels but also went beyond it. In his masterpiece, the *Summa Theologica,* he admitted that "our knowledge of the angels is imperfect" and that therefore "we can only distinguish the angelic offices and orders in a general way." But he added,

> If we knew the offices and distinctions of the angels perfectly, we should know perfectly that each angel has his own office and his own order among things.

Aquinas believed each angel is his own "species" (unlike mankind, which is all one), and that each angel stands alone on his own level in a perfectly ranked ordering of all of them.

Aquinas, by the way, wrote many thousands of words about angels, and was so esteemed for his intellect that in all of history, only he was known by the academic title "Doctor of Angels." But about the time of his forty-ninth birthday he had a vision that redirected his life. This preeminent scholar suddenly stopped writing altogether, and said, "Such things have been revealed to me that all I have written seems as straw." Perhaps he even saw an angel in his vision, and that one glimpse of heavenly reality made his volumes of intellectual discourse seem as nothing by comparison. He died before he reached age fifty.

Aquinas had been influenced and inspired by an earlier writer who went by the name of Dionysius, though his real identity was unknown. In one of his works, *Celestial Hierarchy,* Dionysius pushed forward his detailed ideas of angel organization. A thousand years later John Calvin found reason to suspect the suppositions of Dionysius, and to put the question of angel hierarchy in better perspective.

Calvin wrote,

> None can deny that Dionysius (whoever he may have been) has many shrewd and subtle discussions in his Celestial Hierarchy; but on looking at them more closely, every one must see that they are merely idle talk.

Calvin counseled his readers to "renounce those vain babblings of idle men concerning the nature, ranks, and number of angels, without any authority from the Word of God." He said the path of discipleship taught by Jesus discouraged this kind of "superfluous speculations," and that we, "being contented with him for our master," should do the same.

"When you read the work of Dionysius," Calvin reflected, "you would think that the man had come down from heaven, and was relating not what he had learned but what he had actually seen."

Calvin contrasted that with Paul's example. We know from Scripture that Paul was actually "caught up to the third heaven" and "caught up to paradise" (2 Corinthians 12:2,4). But instead of coming back and chattering about heaven's furnishings or about the setup of the angels there, Paul affirmed simply that he had encountered "inexpressible things, things that man is not permitted to tell" (12:4). Paul, whom we assume could have shared many secrets about angelic arrangement, instead was constrained to silence.

In the centuries leading up to Jesus' ministry on earth and the birth of the Church, many popular ideas of extensive angelic organization had developed among the Jews. They conjectured a variety of angelic positions and functions. Paul may have had this in mind when he said Christ is seated "far above" not only "all rule and authority, power and dominion," but also above "every title that *can be given*" (Ephesians 1:21). We can strain our imaginations to the breaking point in describing multi-layers of angelic superstructure, but it doesn't matter. Regardless of how dignified and dazzling and detailed the angel forces may be, and regardless of how powerful and wonderful angels will appear when we see them in the age to come, their glory is always as darkness compared to Christ. And Christ is all that matters.

Order and Harmony

Nevertheless there's something worth learning from angels when Scripture calls them by these exalted titles. Calvin himself was willing to say the terms *powers, authorities,* and *rulers* indicated that God's government of this world "is exercised and administered" by angels. To him these words also show "the dignity of angelic service."

As for the name *thrones,* Calvin said perhaps it's used for angels "because the glory of God in some measure dwells in them." But with typical caution Calvin hastened to add, "As to this last designation I am unwilling to speak positively, as a different interpretation is equally if not more congruous."

So the Scriptures don't make a big deal of a detailed angelic organization, but they do seem to allow for it.

It makes sense that there's order and organization among the angels, "for God is not a God of disorder but of peace" (1 Corinthians 14:33). Throughout God's visible creation, even amid all the wondrous variety of it, we see an amazing orderliness, a profusion of patterns all interlocking with symmetry and logic. It's a master design that brings glory to the Master Designer, because he not only made it but also sustains it. It's his active energy that keeps it running moment by moment and season after season.

It seems only reasonable that the angelic realm, which God also created and sustains, is just as masterfully designed, however limited we are now in understanding it.

So what difference should all that make to you and me? Why should we care whether the angel domain is well-ordered and humming smoothly? For that matter, why should we care whether nature is well-ordered and humming smoothly?

Our first concern should be to recognize that this orderliness is a reflection on God. We learn about him from what we see in the creation which he made and continues to hold together. Creation is complex and intricate and harmonious and orderly because that's the way God is.

Our second focus should be on ourselves. Unlike the angels and nature, we human beings have deliberately turned away from God's original design for us. So now we have to go through the struggle of rediscovering that orderly design, then understanding and applying it.

Let's ask some hard, specific questions: Have we really recognized the master design God set up for our churches? Do we understand it, as proved by the fact that we're living it out in peace and harmony?

And the same at home: Have we really recognized the master design God set up for our families? Do we prove we understand it by the way we live it out in peace and harmony?

Yes, orderliness is just as important in church and at home as it is in nature and in the angelic sphere.

Satan understands this, which is why he constantly attacks the God-ordained chain of love and authority established for our churches and our homes. Whenever there's disorder in these places, someone other than God is behind it, because God is not the author of confusion.

Are you experiencing disorder now in your home or church? If so, can you pinpoint the ways God's design is being overlooked or opposed?

And how about your personal life, your inner reality? God is not a God of disorder but of peace. Is peace the dominant note inside you, or has it been disrupted by disorder and confusion and instability?

Spirituality implies an orderliness in our lives.

Hosts and Chariots

Another name we've seen used for angels collectively is "hosts." We discovered earlier that this one's especially important because of God's personal identification with it—he so often calls himself "the Lord of Hosts."

This word *hosts* also implies order and organization among the angels, especially in the sense that angels are organized for battle. It's a military picture. *Hosts* is the primary scriptural word for God's heavenly armies. We can picture well-trained troops, their loyalty unquestioned, their obedience

instantaneous. They're in perpetual readiness to respond to their Commander's call. Angels must surely be more tightly ordered than any army, any
military machine on earth.

Angels are called hosts, Calvin writes,

> because they surround their Prince as his court—they adorn and
> display his majesty. Like soldiers they have their eyes always turned
> to their leader's standard, and are so ready and prompt to execute his
> orders that the moment he gives the nod they prepare for work, or
> rather are actually at it.

The name "Lord of Hosts" for God is first used at a military low-point
in Israel's history—at the beginning of First Samuel (1:3), which opens at a
period when the Philistines were oppressing God's people. Matthew Henry
says this title of God was probably introduced by the prophet Samuel here
"for the comfort of Israel" at a time when "their hosts were few and feeble
and those of their enemies many and mighty."

This name would soon be encouragement indeed to a shepherd boy
called David. He shouted to his mighty Philistine enemy Goliath,

> You come against me with sword and spear and javelin, but I come
> against you *in the name of the Lord of Hosts, the God of the armies of
> Israel,* whom you have defied. (1 Samuel 17:45)

With the honor and presence of the Lord of Hosts on their side, Israel
won the battle that day.

But they lost another one centuries later when a king was determined
to lead his soldiers into battle without the Lord and his hosts on the king's
side. Not that Israel's King Ahab wasn't warned. The prophet Micaiah stood
before him and said, "I saw the Lord sitting on his throne with *all the host of
heaven* standing on his right and on his left" (2 Chronicles 18:18). And what
were God and all these angels discussing? Not how to give victory to Ahab,
but how to bring disaster and death to this corrupt ruler (18:19-22).

Ahab refused to heed Micaiah's vision. His men charged into battle against the Syrians, and the king was wounded when a randomly shot arrow pierced him between the sections of his armor. Ahab propped himself up in his chariot to see the rest of the day's battle, while his blood covered the chariot floor. He died at sunset, as the battle turned against Israel.

The strategies of God and his armies can never be thwarted.

We saw earlier how this military side of the Lord and his hosts is strong enough that sometimes the presence of angels need only be implied by mentioning their chariots. We heard David's song of praise: "The chariots of God are tens of thousands and thousands of thousands" (Psalm 68:17). We heard Isaiah's warning: 'See, the Lord is coming with fire, and his chariots are like a whirlwind" (66:15-16). We saw God answering Elisha's prayer by opening up his servant's eyes to see "the hills full of horses and chariots of fire all around" (2 Kings 6:17). Even the "chariot of fire and horses of fire" that swooped down to carry Elijah to heaven were most likely an angel squadron on special assignment: to bring an old soldier home (2 Kings 2:11-12).

This military aspect of the angels is as much an example for us as is their orderliness. When David shouts to the Lord, *"Your troops* will be willing on your day of battle" (Psalm 110:3), both angels and men may well be the Lord's ready soldiers on that day.

Are you his willing soldier? The more you learn about angels—the more clearly you see what spiritual reality in this universe is all about—the more you'll hear the call to arms. For heavenly battle lines are drawn, and you and I cannot escape the fight. We must be steeled for the fray.

> Put on God's complete armor so that you can successfully resist all the devil's craftiness. For our fight is not against any physical enemy; it is against organizations and powers that are spiritual. We are up against the unseen power that controls this dark world, and spiritual

agents from the very headquarters of evil. Therefore *you must wear the whole armor of God.*... (Ephesians 6:11-13, J. B. Phillips)

Hear the trumpet's alarm! "Be on your guard; stand firm in the faith; be men of courage; be strong" (1 Corinthians 16:13). Victory is assured (won by Christ himself!) and you have only to stand and see it. But you can't even do that if you're defenseless, if you're a naked target for the enemy. Don't leave yourself open to a fall! Strap on the Lord's full armor, "that when the day of evil comes, you may be able to stand your ground, and after you have done everything, *to stand*" (Ephesians 6:13).

This is warfare like no other. So go for the best protection there is:

Put on *the armor of light.*...
Clothe yourselves with *the Lord Jesus Christ.*... (Romans 13:12-14)

Holy Ones

Remember: Names *mean* something in the Bible. With that in mind let's look at more Scripture names for angels. Some of these may refer to all God's angels and others only to special classes of them.

Angels are called "holy ones." They're separated, set apart for God's use. This holiness *comes* from God's holiness and *points* to God's holiness. A statement about them in Psalm 89:7 is a strong picture of this:

In the council of *the holy ones* God is greatly feared;
he is more awesome than all who surround him.

The angels assembled around God are holy. But their awesome holiness doesn't compare with God's, so the angels "greatly fear" him.

"Holy ones" is also what the angels are called when Moses describes them coming to Mount Sinai when God gave the law to Israel (Deuteronomy 33:2). Job's friend Eliphaz calls angels "holy ones" (Job 5:1, 15:15). So does Daniel in recounting his visions:

Then I heard *a holy one* speaking, and *another holy one* said to him, "How long will it take for the vision to be fulfilled...? (Daniel 8:13)

Notice how in three other passages—one in the Old Testament and two in the New—the Lord is seen as "coming with his holy ones" on some future day. In all three verses the "holy ones" mentioned may refer to both redeemed believers and unfallen angels:

You will flee as you fled from the earthquake in the days of Uzziah king of Judah. Then *the Lord my God will come, and all the holy ones with him.* (Zechariah 14:5)

May he strengthen your hearts so that you will be blameless and holy in the presence of our God and Father when *our Lord Jesus comes with all his holy ones.* (1 Thessalonians 3:13)

See, *the Lord is coming with thousands upon thousands of his holy ones* to judge everyone, and to convict all the ungodly of all the ungodly acts they have done in the ungodly way, and of all the harsh words ungodly sinners have spoken against him. (Jude 14-15)

Once again our human destiny is linked with angels.

Mighty Ones of God

Emphasizing their power, angels are even called "gods" and "sons of God" and "sons of the mighty." Just as their holiness does their might points back to God. The King James Version of Psalm 89:6 captures this well: "Who among *the sons of the mighty* can be likened unto the Lord?" Angels are mighty, but their might is nothing compared with God's.

The angels must surely follow with gladness what David says to them:

Ascribe to the Lord, *O mighty ones,*
    ascribe to the Lord glory and strength. (Psalm 29:1)

> Praise the Lord, you his angels,
>
> you *mighty ones* who do his bidding,
>
> who obey his word. (103:20)

In Psalm 8:5, where David says that man was made only "a little lower than the heavenly beings," the Hebrew word for these beings is actually the word *elohim* or "gods." We see their exalted power but also their reflection of God's glory. Calvin says angels are "more than once called gods, because the Deity is in some measure represented to us in their service, as in a mirror."

We can see another measure of divine power mirrored in the angels of Revelation. John saw and heard "a *mighty* angel" asking in God's throne-room, "Who is worthy to break the seals and open the scroll?" (5:2). It's "another *mighty* angel" who "planted his right foot on the sea and his left foot on the land" (10:1-2). And it's "a *mighty* angel" who "picked up a boulder the size of a large millstone and threw it into the sea" (18:21).

In 2 Thessalonians 1:7, Paul says the Lord Jesus will be "revealed from heaven in blazing fire with his *powerful angels.*" Bible scholars say this last phrase might best be translated as *"the angels of his power."* It could refer to a special group of angels with special power from God, or it could be another way of showing the great power all his angels have.

Holy Watchers

A different perspective on angels comes through when we see them referred to as "watchers" by King Nebuchadnezzar as he talked with Daniel, his royal advisor. The Hebrew word translated here as "watchers" or "watchmen" (or "messengers" in some versions) is used nowhere in the Bible except in Daniel 4. It comes from a verb meaning "to be wakeful" and "on the watch."

Nebuchadnezzar was telling Daniel about a dream he'd had while in bed in his palace, "contented and prosperous" (4:4). In that dream he saw a large, healthy, fruitful tree with birds in its branches and animals resting in its shade.

> I was looking in the visions in my mind as I lay on my bed, and behold, an angelic *watcher,* a holy one, descended from heaven. (4:13, NASB)

This holy watcher from heaven gave orders for the tree to be cut down, and the stump and the roots bound with iron. The watcher also described someone (it turns out to be the king himself) who was sentenced to being "drenched with the dew," living outside with animals, and having an animal's mind. "This sentence," said the watcher,

> is by the decree of the angelic *watchers,* and the decision is a command of the holy ones. (4:17, NASB)

So there were other "watchers" besides the one talking to Nebuchadnezzar, and they were entrusted in some manner with pronouncing God's judgment. They could be a particular class of angels with special duty related to communicating God's decrees.

In Nebuchadnezzar's case the watcher gave the reason for this particular verdict:

> so that the living may know that the Most High is sovereign over the kingdoms of men and gives them to anyone he wishes and sets over them the lowliest of men.

Nebuchadnezzar became that "lowliest of men" as he took on an animal's existence, living outdoors and eating grass. His hair grew out and his unclipped nails became like claws. When God finally restored his sanity, Nebuchadnezzar was ready to give honor and glory to God as the one who "does as he pleases with the powers of heaven and the peoples of the earth" (4:35).

The watchers were right.

Cherubim and God's Throne

The background of the name *cherub* is something of a mystery. Some scholars suggest that it's related to words meaning "intercessor" or "guardian." Others see a connection to words meaning "to grasp or hold fast," or "to plow or till the ground" or "to be diligent." Perhaps cherubim (the Hebrew plural of *cherub*) are the real workhorses among the angels as they fulfill their role as royal guards in service to the King. For sure they're a far cry from naked valentine babies.

We originally encountered cherubim in Genesis 3 as the first angelic beings mentioned in Scripture. Cherubim guarded Eden's gate with a flaming sword after Adam's fall, showing us vividly that sin can never be a part of paradise.

The next mention of cherubim is when God is giving Moses directions for making the ark of the covenant and the tabernacle. The ark was to have a pure gold "atonement cover" or "mercy seat" on top, and this cover included two hammered-gold cherubim. The author of Hebrews calls them "cherubim of the Glory" (9:5).

Note the reverent pose God told Moses to give these figures:

> The cherubim are to have their wings spread upward, overshadowing the cover with them. The cherubim are to face each other, looking toward the cover. (Exodus 25:20)

Since the ark represented God's throne and his royal presence, the gold cherubim figures with upraised wings remind us that God on his throne is surrounded by glorious, worshiping angels. Their faces turned toward the "atonement cover" or "mercy seat"—which itself is suggestive of Christ's atoning sacrifice—could indicate that the destiny of angels is also caught up in what Christ accomplished on the cross. Or it might be a strong picture of the angels "longing to look" into the things of salvation (1 Peter 1:12).

Or perhaps, as some scholars venture to say, the cherubim are a picture of the ideal future state of redeemed mankind, and their gaze at the mercy seat represents their eternal gratitude and praise for Christ's sacrifice. The cherubim are what *we* might be like someday.

This cherubim motif was carefully repeated in other tabernacle furnishings as well. The Lord commanded that ten tabernacle curtains be made "of finely twisted linen and blue, purple and scarlet yarn, *with cherubim worked into them* by a skilled craftsman" (Exodus 26:1). A curtain dividing the inner chambers of the tabernacle was also to have "*cherubim worked into it* by a skilled craftsman" (26:31).

In connection with the cherubim-shadowed ark, God promised his presence to Moses:

> There, above the cover *between the two cherubim* that are over the ark of the Testimony, *I will meet with you* and give you all my commands for the Israelites. (25:22)

God right away made good on this promise:

> When Moses entered the Tent of Meeting to speak with the Lord, he heard the voice speaking to him *from between the two cherubim* above the atonement cover on the ark of the Testimony. And he spoke with him. (Numbers 7:89)

From then on many in Israel remembered this sign of the Lord's presence and earthly kingship among them, for God was often called the one "enthroned between the cherubim" (1 Samuel 4:4, 2 Samuel 6:2, 2 Kings 19:15, 1 Chronicles 13:6, Psalm 80:1, 99:1).

When a massive Assyrian army was camped outside Jerusalem waiting to destroy it, King Hezekiah began his prayer this way: "O Lord of Hosts, God of Israel, *enthroned between the cherubim*, you alone are God over all the kingdoms of the earth…" (Isaiah 37:16). It was in answer to this prayer that the angel of the Lord put to death 185,000 Assyrian soldiers in a single night.

A different glimpse of the cherubim comes in David's song of praise and victory in 2 Samuel 22, "when the Lord delivered him from the hand of all his enemies and from the hand of Saul." It's an amazing picture of the cherubim actually carrying God's presence down to David's rescue:

> He parted the heavens and came down;
>> dark clouds were under his feet.
> *He mounted the cherubim* and flew;
>> he soared on the wings of the wind. (22:10-11)

Since the cherubim signify the angelic presence around God's throne, David felt that when the Lord rescued him it was just as if God had packed up his heavenly throne and come down with it to be the liberating King in David's life.

You and I can have that same picture of our own situation. We can be confident of God's kingly help coming to our rescue exactly when needed:

> Let us then approach *the throne of grace* with confidence, so that we may receive mercy and find grace to help us in our time of need. (Hebrews 4:16)

Yes, "The Lord is our king; it is he who will save us" (Isaiah 33:22).

Cherubim in the Temple

When David's son Solomon built the temple to replace the tabernacle, cherubim were again featured in the furnishing, but this time even more so.

The temple followed closely the pattern God had shown Moses for the tabernacle. In 1 Chronicles 28:11-12 we learn that David gave his son Solomon the plans for every part of the temple, and these were plans "that the Spirit had put in his mind." That's important to remember. The figures of cherubim adorning the tabernacle and the temple were *God's* idea—they were not human-conceived decorations.

Imagine yourself being there in Solomon's reign, some three thousand years ago. You're walking up the steps before the east entrance of the new temple, the world's most famous building. To visitors from other lands this is the centerpiece in the capital city of the world's wisest and richest king. But it means much more than that to you and your countrymen. This is the chosen earthly dwelling of the Lord of Hosts, and today is his Day of Atonement. Today is the only day of the year that *any* person can enter into the Most Holy Place—the Holy of Holies.

And you are that person, for you are the high priest.

You and your fellow priests have already offered the special sacrifices for this day upon the great altar in front of the temple. Now you carry a golden bowl filled with the blood of a goat that was slaughtered as a special sin offering for the people. You are to take this blood inside the Holy of Holies and sprinkle it on the atonement cover on the Ark of the Covenant.

At the top of the steps you walk between two giant cast-bronze pillars into a portico. Before you are two huge doors. Carved into them are intricately formed figures of cherubim. Your eyes go at once to their wings, then to their lion-like shoulders, then to their solemn, mysterious faces. All these features are highlighted in hammered gold, glittering in the brilliant midday sun of Israel. As you look long into one of their faces, suddenly a chill runs down your neck. With a twinge of terror you imagine the reality of their presence at God's home in heaven.

Bravely you reach out a hand. One of the doors swings back smoothly to your touch. You hold your breath. You sense that the cherubim on the open door are watching as you enter a large room.

A gold-covered floor gleams before you. Away on either side are gold-covered walls soaring up nearly fifty feet. The light from golden lampstands on both sides of the room reflects off the carvings covering the walls— countless more cherubim. Their awesome forms are set off with palm trees and flowers, all covered in gold. You stand for several moments staring at one cherub, then another, and another. Each one seems alive. You almost fear to go forward.

Finally you move. Your bare feet step slowly and silently across sixty feet of golden floor until you stand before a square, gold-covered altar. The smoke of sacred incense rises from it.

Behind the altar two more gold-covered doors tower above you, and these too are covered with carved cherubim, plus palm trees and flowers. You kneel before the incense altar and pray, then stand again and step behind the altar.

You reach out to touch one of the cherubim-covered doors. You close your eyes. Only after you swing both doors open wide do you open your eyes as well—to gaze upon this, a room untouched and unseen for a full year: the inner sanctuary, the Holy of Holies.

The gleaming light from the main hall pours in through the doorway into the gold-covered sanctuary. Facing you and towering above you are two gleaming statues of magnificent golden cherubim, each one fifteen feet high. Their wings are raised up and out. Their outer wings touch the wall. Their inner wings touch one another, forming an arch, fifteen feet across. Below the winged arch is the Ark of the Covenant, with its atonement cover— where two more cherubim with outstretched wings overshadow the Ark.

In the silent majesty of that room you feel your hands and legs quivering. You fall to your knees. The familiar opening of the ninety-ninth psalm leaps from your heart to your lips:

> The Lord reigns,
>   let the nations tremble;
> *he sits enthroned between the cherubim,*
>   let the earth shake.

Centuries later the Babylonians destroyed this beautiful temple. The grieving Jews must have had those beautiful cherubim-covered walls in mind in Psalm 74 as they lamented what the invaders had done:

They behaved like men wielding axes
    to cut through a thicket of trees.
They smashed all the carved paneling
    with their axes and hatchets.
They burned your sanctuary to the ground;
    they defiled the dwelling place of your Name.

But already the vision of a new temple was given to the priest and prophet Ezekiel, who was with the Jewish exiles in Babylon. The new temple would also be filled from floor to ceiling with cherubim "at regular intervals all around the inner and outer sanctuary" (Ezekiel 41:17), and interspersed again with palm trees. This is what the cherubim looked like:

Each cherub had two faces: the face of a man toward the palm tree on one side and the face of a lion toward the palm tree on the other. (41:18-19)

And once more the doors to the sanctuary would be filled with "carved cherubim and palm trees like those carved on the walls" (41:25).

But even in this exalted vision, the sight of those cherubim probably would not have been quite as awesome to Ezekiel as they would be to you or me—because not long before, Ezekiel had been privileged to see *the real thing.* God opened the heavens and gave to Ezekiel a vision of his throne and the cherubim surrounding it.

The power and beauty of these angelic beings cannot be fully conveyed within the limits of human language, but Ezekiel does the best he can. His descriptions in Ezekiel 1 push us beyond human imagination, yet they include much detail. It's worth our while to include nearly all this chapter here with its awesome presentation of these heavenly beings. (Ezekiel first calls them "living creatures," and not until chapter ten are they identified as cherubim.)

First the scene for the vision. Ezekiel sees

a windstorm coming out of the north—an immense cloud with flashing lightning and surrounded by brilliant light. The center of the fire looked like glowing metal, and in the fire was what looked like *four living creatures.*

What stands out first to Ezekiel is their faces, their wings, and their fire.

In appearance their form was that of a man, but each of them had four faces and four wings. Their legs were straight; their feet were like those of a calf and gleamed like burnished bronze. Under their wings on their four sides they had the hands of a man. *All four of them had faces and wings,* and their wings touched one another....

Their *faces* looked like this: Each of the four had the face of a man, and on the right side each had the face of a lion, and on the left the face of an ox; each also had the face of an eagle. Such were their faces.

Their *wings* were spread out upward; each had two wings, one touching the wing of another creature on either side, and two wings covering its body....

The appearance of the living creatures was *like burning coals of fire or like torches.* Fire moved back and forth among the creatures; it was bright, and lightning flashed out of it.

Ezekiel also is fascinated by their movements:

Each one went straight ahead; they did not turn as they moved....

Each one went straight ahead. Wherever the spirit would go, they would go, without turning as they went....

The creatures sped back and forth like flashes of lightning.

Then he sees a spellbinding dance-like motion of sparkling, intersecting wheels full of eyes. But notice how the wheels are not independent of the living creatures, but somehow are spiritually a part of them. Try to imagine the sight:

As I looked at the living creatures, I saw a wheel on the ground
beside each creature with its four faces. This was the appearance and
structure of the wheels: They sparkled like chrysolite, and all four
looked alike. Each appeared to be made like a wheel intersecting a
wheel.... Their rims were high and awesome, and all four rims were
full of eyes all around.

When the living creatures moved, the wheels beside them moved;
and when the living creatures rose from the ground, the wheels also
rose. Wherever the spirit would go, they would go, and the wheels
would rise along with them, because the spirit of the living creatures
was in the wheels. When the creatures moved, they also moved;
when the creatures stood still, they also stood still; and when the
creatures rose from the ground, the wheels rose along with them,
because the spirit of the living creatures was in the wheels.

Ezekiel also lets us hear with his ears:

When the creatures moved, I heard the sound of their wings, like the
roar of rushing waters, like the voice of the Almighty, like the tumult
of an army.

God's angels always point us to God, and that now becomes clear in
Ezekiel's case as well. He isn't being shown this vision just to learn about
cherubim, but rather to hear a word from the Lord.

Ezekiel glances "above the heads of the living creatures" and sees "what
looked like an expanse, sparkling like ice, and awesome." He hears a voice
from the expanse, then looks up to see this overwhelming vision:

Above the expanse over their heads was what looked like a throne of
sapphire, and high above on the throne was a figure like that of a
man.... From what appeared to be his waist up he looked like glowing metal, as if full of fire... and from there down he looked like fire;

and brilliant light surrounded him. Like the appearance of a rainbow in the clouds on a rainy day, so was the radiance around him.

This was the appearance of the likeness of the glory of the Lord. When I saw it, I fell facedown, and I heard the voice of one speaking.

After all these preliminaries, God now gives Ezekiel his calling and instructions, as recorded in Ezekiel 2 and 3.

Ezekiel must have recalled this vision every day for the rest of his life as he faced the struggles and pressures of living out his calling. It must have brought constant motivation and encouragement to think that this was the God he served.

How many of us would enjoy having had a majestic and mysterious vision like that to keep us going in our own specific calling from God? But the fact is, we *do* have it. Through his Word the Lord has given it to us for keeps. The God whom Ezekiel saw surrounded and served by flaming cherubim will always be the same. Ezekiel's vision is for you and me even more than it was for Ezekiel.

In Scripture we never see the cherubim serving as messengers from God to men—at least by their words. But their appearance must have communicated a great deal to Ezekiel, to God's people who saw the figures in the temple and tabernacle, and to Adam and Eve fleeing from Eden.

Seraphim

The name *seraph* means "burning one" or "shining one" (reminding us again that God makes his angels "flames of fire"—Psalm 104:4, Hebrews 1:7). The seraphim dwell so close to the presence of God that they burn with holy brilliance.

They are mentioned by name in only one passage in the Bible, but what an awesome scene it is. Let's return again to the vision where Isaiah sees God on his throne and hears voices around him crying "Holy, holy, holy is the Lord of Hosts" (Isaiah 6:1-4).

Isaiah says these are seraphs who sound that continual praise. He describes them as having six wings. With two wings they cover their faces in reverence. This reminds us of God's majestic glory. The Bible says no man has ever seen God and lived, and even these angels protect themselves from the brilliance of God's glory when they're in his presence. Matthew Henry expressed it this way:

> Though angels' faces doubtless are much fairer than those of the children of men (Acts 6:15), yet in the presence of God they cover them because they cannot bear the dazzling luster of the divine glory, and because, being conscious of an infinite distance from the divine perfection, they are ashamed to show their faces before the holy God.

Isaiah notices also that with two other wings the seraphs cover their feet. This speaks of their humility and their reverence in waiting on God for his next directions.

With their other two wings the seraphs fly. These two wings propel them with speed to do whatever God calls them to do.

Notice the proportion: Four wings for worship and only two for work—twice as much attention to being in God's presence as compared to carrying out other responsibilities. It seems like we today often reverse this ratio. We would do well to be more like the seraphim.

Like Ezekiel's vision of the cherubim, Isaiah's vision of the seraphim provides another picture of reverence and adoring awe to help us in approaching our heavenly Father. Trying to follow their example in this may seem uncomfortable and even threatening. But if it felt only cozy and comfortable, God would not be God.

Isaiah knew this tension. While the seraphs sang "Holy, holy, holy," he was thinking how much he was "unholy, unholy, unholy." He cried out, "Woe, I am ruined!" (6:5). But through the touch of a live coal from a seraph's hand to Isaiah's lips, the prophet was able to continue in his encounter with the holy God. The Lord will give the right grace for us to do it too.

Just as in Ezekiel's case, Isaiah after this experience was able at once to hear God's specific calling. Isaiah responded gladly. "Here am I," he said. "Send me!" Our own understanding of God's will for our lives will open up as well after an extended experience of worship in the fear of God.

Living Creatures and Elders

At the end of Scripture, in John's vision on Patmos Island, he saw "four living creatures" who have similarities to both the seraphim in Isaiah 6 and the cherubim in Ezekiel 1. Their name—"living creatures"—quickly tells us that they have life and that they're created beings.

Like the cherubim, these living creatures number four and have the likenesses of lion, ox, man, and eagle (Revelation 4:7). And like the seraphim they have six wings, and honor God with their continual praise of "Holy, holy, holy is the Lord God Almighty"—to which they add a new phrase: "who was, and is, and is to come" (4:8).

They're able to praise God in this new way because of two things which we learn about them right away. The first is that in God's presence they stand *"in the center,* around the throne" (4:6). They may well be closer to God than any other angelic beings.

The second thing we learn about them is that they're "covered with eyes, in front and in back," reminding us of the cherubim's wheels in Ezekiel 1, which had eyes all along the rims. These living creatures in Revelation are fully alive to see everything, past and future, front and back. Perhaps they can actually *see* that God was, and is, and is to come.

The four living creatures are involved not only in worshiping God but also in bringing about his final wrath upon the earth. As John watches the Lamb opening the first of the seven seals, he says,

I heard one of the four living creatures say in a voice like thunder, "Come!" (6:1)

This authoritative shout summons a rider on a white horse who "rode out as a conqueror bent on conquest" (6:2). As Christ opens the next three seals, the other three creatures each in turn also calls out, "Come!" Again their simple command immediately brings forth a horse and rider bearing destruction to the earth. The living creatures know how to make their words count.

Later John says he saw

seven angels with the seven plagues…. Then *one of the four living creatures* gave to the seven angels seven golden bowls filled with the wrath of God, who lives for ever and ever. (15:6-7)

Closely associated with the four living creatures in Revelation are the "twenty-four elders." When John first sees them they're seated on twenty-four thrones that encircle God's throne. "They were dressed in white and had crowns of gold on their heads" (4:4).

This name *elders* implies "leadership by example." These elders are like our "older examples," the ones we look up to as models for our behavior. As "elders" they bear the same name that the highest Scripture-ordained leaders of our churches have. So perhaps their worship and service to God is especially meant to be an example to those in church leadership—who in turn are meant to be "examples to the flock" (1 Peter 5:3).

The elders in Revelation are especially involved in proclaiming God's saving acts toward men. One of their most glorious moments is when "the seventh angel sounded his trumpet" (11:15) and loud heavenly voices announce that at last the world is completely and forever under the reign of Christ.

The elders are now in John's focus, setting the example for the rest of us in responding to Christ's kingship: "The twenty-four elders, who were

seated on their thrones before God, fell on their faces and worshiped God."
Just listen to their praise (in 11:17-18), and how it involves you and me and
all the Christians we know, small and great:

> We give thanks to you, Lord God Almighty,
>> the One who is and who was,
> because you have taken your great power
>> and have begun to reign.
> The nations were angry;
>> and your wrath has come.
> The time has come for judging the dead,
>> and for rewarding your servants the prophets
> and your saints and those who reverence your name,
>> both small and great—
> and for destroying those who destroy the earth.

Notice the assurance here that God *will* take care of us! The elders know
this, and they want us to know it as well.

Now look what happens next—and let your mind recall those cherubim in the temple and what they represented:

> Then God's temple in heaven was opened, and within his temple was
> seen the ark of his covenant. And there came flashes of lightning,
> rumblings, peals of thunder, an earthquake and a great hailstorm.

These elders definitely know what it means to get a response when they
worship! No wonder they love doing it all the time.

We see the elders and the four living creatures worshiping together
often—in fact we could almost say the living creatures set the pace as
heaven's worship leaders, while the twenty-four elders are their assistants
showing us how to rightly respond. An example is in 4:9-10.

Whenever the living creatures give glory, honor and thanks to him who sits on the throne and who lives for ever and ever *the twenty-four elders* fall down before him who sits on the throne, and worship him who lives for ever and ever.

At this point the elders "lay their crowns before the throne" and praise God for his worthiness as Creator and Sustainer of all things. What an example for us—actually setting aside their own honor (their crowns) in order to give more glory to the One who alone is worthy of it all.

Notice also the elders and the living creatures working together in the scene with the unopened scroll in Revelation 5—when John was weeping "because no one was found who was worthy to open the scroll." It was "one of the elders" who told John to stop crying, and turned his attention to Christ. Then John saw the slain Lamb "standing in the center of the throne, encircled by the four living creatures and the elders" (5:6).

After Christ had taken the scroll from God's hand,

the four living creatures and *the twenty-four elders* fell down before the Lamb. Each one had a harp and they were holding golden bowls full of incense, which are the prayers of the saints. And they sang a new song: "You are worthy to take the scroll and to open its seals, because you were slain, and with your blood you purchased men for God...." (5:8-9)

The scene reaches a climax when "every creature in heaven and on earth and under the earth" sings praise to God and to the Lamb (5:13). Then look again at our worship team in action:

The four living creatures said, "Amen," and *the elders* fell down and worshiped. (5:14)

And after that "Amen" I'm sure everyone there was feeling, "What a wonderful worship service we've had!" It couldn't be better.

If these heavenly beings really will be our future worship leaders up there, isn't it great that God's already introduced them to us?

Meanwhile let's meet some particular angels one by one. "One by one" is actually as far as we can go right now, because only two angels in Scripture are individually named. Both are justifiably famous.

Gabriel

Gabriel's name means "Mighty One of God." Gabriel would probably easily win the award for "Most Admired Angel." He always seems to be bringing important news, and usually quite good news.

Gabriel met Zechariah inside the Holy of Holies in the temple to tell him that his prayers had been answered (that's always good news!) and that he would have a son. And not just any son, but the forerunner of the Christ (Luke 1:11-17).

Shortly afterward Gabriel went to a girl named Mary to tell her the best news the world has ever heard: God was sending his Son to earth in the flesh, to establish a kingdom that would never end (1:26-37).

Five hundred years earlier, the news Gabriel brought to Daniel was more complicated, with its visions of future world-shaking events. But his welcome word to Daniel in 9:23 reminds us of the news Zechariah heard and that we all long to hear—"As soon as you began to pray, an answer was given...."

Gabriel has good news to give because he stays in the right place to learn it. As he told Zechariah, "I am Gabriel. *I stand in the presence of God.*" If you want good news to give people you love, stay long in the presence of God.

No doubt Gabriel will be quite an awesome sight for us to behold in heaven, but when he came to Daniel he seems to have taken on a more normal human aspect. Daniel says he "looked like a man" (8:15), and later calls him "the man I had seen in the earlier vision" (9:21).

Gabriel is perfect at the job of being God's messenger. Notice how concisely and helpfully he explains to Daniel what he's up to: "I am going *to tell you* what will happen later," he says in 8:19. And on his next visit he says,

> Daniel, I have now come *to give you insight and understanding.* As soon as you began to pray, an answer was given, which I have come *to tell you....* (9:22-23)

Likewise he makes his mission plain to Zechariah:

> I stand in the presence of God, and I have been sent to speak to you and to tell you this good news. (Luke 1:19)

He also knows how to be positive and encouraging, a great skill to have in communication. He tells Daniel, "You are highly esteemed" (9:23). And listen to his encouragement for Mary:

> Greetings, you who are highly favored! The Lord is with you....Do not be afraid, Mary, you have found favor with God. (Luke 1:28-30)

Gabriel is also quite a mover. Daniel tells us, "While I was still in prayer, Gabriel...came to me *in swift flight* about the time of the evening sacrifice" (9:21).

Michael

Michael's name means "Who Is Like God?" While Gabriel is more of an announcing and preaching angel, Michael is more involved in protecting and fighting. Even individual angels seem to have their special gifts and responsibilities, just as members of the body of Christ do.

In Revelation, for example, besides seeing Michael at his task of fighting, we read of an angel "who had charge of the fire" (14:18), "the angel in charge of the waters" (16:5), and an angel who had "the key to the Abyss" (20:1). Apparently angels and believers alike all have their own perfect jobs in carrying out God's perfect will.

Only three times in the Scripture do we see this particular Michael mentioned (there are other Michaels in the Old Testament, but they're men, not angels).

Michael is a royal champion of God's people Israel. He's referred to three times in Daniel, and his tagline gets progressively more exalted and more personal toward Israel:

First he's called "one of the chief princes" in 10:13.

Then it's "Michael, *your* prince" in 10:21.

Finally it's "Michael, the great prince who protects your people" in 12:1.

In the New Testament, Michael is mentioned twice. In Revelation 12:7 he's the leading warrior in the great heavenly battle against Satan—"And there was war in heaven. Michael and his angels fought against the dragon, and the dragon and his angels fought back."

In Jude 9 he's called "the archangel Michael." This title "archangel" means the angel who is "first, principal, chief." Only Michael is given that name in Scripture (Gabriel isn't), and so Paul may be referring to Michael as "*the* archangel" in 1 Thessalonians 4:16—

> For the Lord himself will come down from heaven, with a loud command, with the voice of *the archangel* and with the trumpet call of God, and the dead in Christ will rise first.

Michael's voice may be the one we'll hear on the day of the rapture.

Is Michael the one angel who is above all others? He may well be, though the reference to him in Daniel 10 as *"one of* the chief princes" is enough to keep us from being dogmatic about it. Revelation 8:2 speaks of *"the* seven angels who stand before God." If these are the seven leading angels, it's possible that Michael is one of them and perhaps even the chief of the seven. This is all another mystery we'll learn more about later.

If Michael is the foremost of all angels, then his name is quite appropriate—"Who Is Like God?" The answer, of course, is "No one." Nobody compares to God, not even the mighty captain of the angelic host. Regardless of the great battles Michael wins, or whatever great things any angels do, our only praise must go to the Lord, "who alone does marvelous deeds" (Psalm 72:18).

Yes, having a name that's meaningful is a great way to let others know what's significant about you. That's certainly the way it is with angels—who are messengers, and powers, and warrior hosts, and holy ones, and mighty ones, and watchers, and hard-working guardians, and burning and shining ones, and living creatures, and elder examples—but still, nothing much in comparison to God.

And what about you and me? Do our names reveal the best truths about us? Of course they do! We're saints, and Christians ("little Christs" or "Christ Ones"), and believers, and brothers and sisters in the Lord, and children of God, and disciples, and—well, and quite a lot more.

But that's all a chapter in another book, by another name.

Chapter Nine

THE GREATEST ANGEL

THERE ARE ANGELS—and then there's The Angel.

Now we come to the greatest mystery of all in our study here together: the one who is called *"the* angel of the Lord."

No doubt you've already noticed that often in an Old Testament passage the "angel" who's speaking is identified directly with God himself. The angel seems not just to be *from* the Lord, but actually to *be* the Lord.

As we walk again through Scripture, let's focus our mental lens on this question: Could this be the Lord himself appearing in these encounters?

God or Angel?

We're back along that desert road where a woman kneels by a spring. She is Hagar, Egyptian maidservant to Sarai, the wife of Abram. Here by the spring *"the angel of the Lord found Hagar"* (Genesis 16:7).

In their conversation the angel makes a promise that sounds straight from God: *"I will so increase your descendants that they will be too numerous to count"* (16:10). As Hagar heard this promise, who did she think she was seeing and hearing? Verse 13 tells us:

> She gave this name to *the Lord* who spoke to her: *"You are the God who sees me,"* for she said, *"I have now seen the One who sees me."*

Was he an angel, or was he God?

Now let's climb Mount Moriah, at a time not many years later. On the mountaintop, following God's instructions, Abraham is about to bring down a knife into the cord-bound body of a boy lying on an altar. It's his beloved son Isaac. Abraham's arm is upraised.

> But *the angel of the Lord* called out to him from heaven, "Abraham! Abraham!… Do not lay a hand on the boy." (22:11-12)

At once the angel tells Abraham, "Now I know that you fear *God*, because you have not withheld from *me* your son, your only son." A grateful Abraham then offers a different sacrifice on the altar—a ram instead of his son. And then:

> The *angel of the Lord* called to Abraham from heaven a second time and said, *"I swear by myself,* declares *the Lord,* that because you have done this and have not withheld your son, your only son, *I will surely bless you…."* (22:15-17)

Was he angel or God?

Years later, Isaac's son Jacob is telling his family about a dream.

> *The angel of God* said to me in the dream, "Jacob." I answered, "Here I am." And he said, "…*I am* the *God* of Bethel, where you anointed a pillar and where you made a vow to *me.* Now leave this land at once and go back to your native land." (Genesis 31:11-13)

Was this an angel in Jacob's dream, or God?

But soon Jacob would do more than dream about this heavenly being. As he followed the angel's instructions and traveled back to his native land, he was camping late one night along the Jabbok River. Earlier that evening he had sent his family and his belongings across the ford of the river. For a God-appointed reason, Jacob stayed behind. "Jacob was left alone, and *a man* wrestled with him till daybreak" (32:24).

Who was this man, this endurance wrestler?

The prophet Hosea tells us that he was an "angel," and Hosea summarizes what happened to Jacob that night: "He struggled with *the angel* and overcame him; he wept and begged for his favor" (12:4).

We get more details in Genesis. When this "man" wrestling with Jacob "saw that he could not overpower him, he touched the socket of Jacob's hip so that his hip was wrenched" (32:25). At daybreak the "man" gave Jacob a new name—Israel, which means, "he struggles *with God*."

Then Jacob said, "Please tell me *your name*." The "man" avoided answering Jacob's question, and instead "he blessed him there."

In the light of the morning sun, Jacob—tired and now limping—said, "I saw *God* face to face, and yet my life was spared."

Was the "man" Jacob saw an angel, or was he God?

Four centuries later, Moses is herding sheep "on the far side of the desert" near Horeb, the mountain of God. "There *the angel of the Lord* appeared to him in flames of fire from within a bush" (Exodus 3:1-2). Then "*God* called to him from within the bush" (3:4). Moses would never forget what this "angel" told him:

> I AM WHO I AM.… This is *my* name forever…. Go, assemble the elders of Israel and say to them, "*The Lord*, the *God* of your fathers— the *God* of Abraham, Isaac and Jacob—appeared to me…." (3:14-16)

God or angel?

Another four centuries later, in an Israelite town called Zorah, "the angel of the Lord" appeared to the barren wife of a man named Manoah. The angel promised her that she would bear a son (he would later be called Samson).

When she told this exciting news to her husband, she described the messenger as "a man of God" who "looked like an angel of God, very awesome. I didn't ask him where he came from, and he didn't tell me his name" (Judges 13:6).

Soon afterward the angel came again. This time Manoah saw him too, but he "did not realize that it was the angel of the Lord" (13:16).

> Then Manoah inquired of the angel of the Lord, "What is your name, so that we may honor you when your word comes true?"
>
> He replied, "Why do you ask *my name?* It is *beyond understanding."* (13:17-18)

Following the angel's instructions, Manoah prepared a burnt offering to offer on a rock altar to the Lord.

> And *the Lord* did an amazing thing while Manoah and his wife watched: As the flame blazed up from the altar toward heaven, *the angel of the Lord* ascended in the flame. Seeing this, Manoah and his wife fell with their faces to the ground. When the angel of the Lord did not show himself again to Manoah and his wife, Manoah realized that *it was the angel of the Lord.*
>
> "We are doomed to die!" he said to his wife. "We have seen *God!"* (13:19-22)

At about the same time, the angel of the Lord even made a kind of cross-country trip across a stretch of Israel to broadcast an urgent message to the entire nation. It was urgent because the people had backslidden so far, neglecting to tear down the pagan altars in the land. God in his mercy went all-out to get his people's attention:

> *The angel of the Lord* went up from Gilgal to Bokim and said, "I brought you up out of Egypt and led you into the land that *I* swore to give to your forefathers.... Yet you have disobeyed *me...."*

As punishment, the angel warned that he would not drive out the pagan peoples from Israel's land, but would leave them to become "thorns in your sides."

When *the angel of the Lord* had spoken these things to all the Israelites, the people wept aloud, and they called that place Bokim [which means "weepers"]. There they offered sacrifices to the *Lord.* (Judges 2:1-5)

And so it happened, again and again in the Old Testament. "The angel of the Lord" came on the scene with reproof or guidance or encouragement. He appeared to Gideon as he threshed wheat in a winepress, and to David at the time of the punishing plague, and to the prophets Elijah and Zechariah, and even to Balaam's donkey. And it was "the angel of the Lord" who went out at night and slaughtered 185,000 Assyrians camped outside Jerusalem.

In these passages, did the people (as well as the donkey) actually see *God?*

But Scripture is clear: *No man or woman can ever see God.* The Lord himself told Moses this in the wilderness: "You cannot see my face," he said, "for *no one may see me* and live" (Exodus 33:20).

Jesus said it too, as he claimed for himself a unique relationship with God: *"No one has seen the Father* except the one who is from God," he told the Jews; "only he has seen the Father" (John 6:46).

Paul's teaching holds consistent with this. He calls the Lord "the invisible God" (Colossians 1:15) and praises him as the one "who lives in unapproachable light, *whom no one has seen or can see"* (1 Timothy 6:16).

The apostle John agrees. *"No one has ever seen God,"* he says twice, first in his gospel (1:18), then in his first epistle (4:12).

Moses carefully reminded the people of Israel that when the Lord's presence came with fire and thunder on Mount Sinai, *"You saw no form of any kind* the day the Lord spoke to you" (Deuteronomy 4:15). God cannot be seen.

So who *was* "the angel of the Lord"?

Though the angel of the Lord seems in some ways to be *distinct* from God, there can be no denying that in some mysterious way he was also clearly identified *with* God and *was* God—and therefore not at all like other angels.

Therefore you might be saying right now that this chapter doesn't even belong in a book about angels. Others would probably agree with you. Lewis Sperry Chafer reminds us that the title "Angel of the Lord"

> belongs only to God and is used in connection with the divine manifestations in the earth and *therefore is in no way to be included in the angelic hosts.*

M. J. Erickson writes,

> It is not possible, then, to draw from the nature of the angel of the Lord inferences that can be applied to all angels.

By looking at the angel of the Lord we're in some definite way looking at God. And God, as we know, is set apart from angels just as he is from all the rest of creation. There's a sense in which the actions and behavior of the angel of the Lord in these amazing passages doesn't tell us any more about angels than it does about our crawly friends the caterpillars.

Yet God in his wisdom does use the word *angel* to identify this particular manifestation of himself in these passages. And since the deepest purpose of the book you hold in your hands isn't just to teach us about angels, but rather to help us learn *through* angels what we can about God himself, let's go ahead and stick with the topic for a few pages.

Could He Be Christ?

The angel of the Lord certainly must be more than just an angel with special credentials. Did God the Father himself somehow come down to be represented in temporary human form?

Or—since the angel of the Lord appears to be both distinct from God in heaven as well as identified with him, and seems to possess his deity—is it possible that this could actually be *Christ?* Did God the Son, the second person of the Trinity, come and walk on earth centuries before he was born a baby in Bethlehem?

Some Bible scholars and teachers have been reluctant to come to that conclusion, especially since the New Testament doesn't clearly insist on it. J. M. Wilson says that of the various proposed explanations for the angel of the Lord, identifying him with God the Son "is certainly the most tempting to the mind." Then he adds,

> Yet it must be remembered that at best these are only conjectures that touch on a great mystery.... The appearances of the angel of the Lord ...culminated in the coming of the Savior, and are thus a foreshadowing of, and a preparation for, the full revelation of God in Jesus Christ. Further than this it is not safe to go.

But over the centuries, many who have searched the Scriptures feel it is safe to go further—including Calvin, who wrote:

> I am rather inclined...to agree with ancient writers, that in those passages wherein it is stated that the angel of the Lord appeared to Abraham, Jacob, and Moses, Christ was that angel.

"According to all the evidence," says C. F. Dickason, the angel of the Lord "seems to be the preincarnate Son."

"Christ," wrote Lewis Sperry Chafer, "is the Angel of Jehovah."

And Billy Graham writes,

> There are no grounds for questioning the very early and traditional Christian interpretation that in these cases there is a preincarnation manifestation of the second person of the Trinity.

But rather than take someone else's word for it, let's look at some of the evidence ourselves.

First of all we know that Christ is indeed eternal. His existence did not begin at Bethlehem. He was "with God in the beginning" (John 1:2). "Before Abraham was born, I am!" he told the Jews (8:58). He had glory in God's presence "before the world began" (17:5), and a loving relationship with his Father "before the creation of the world" (17:24).

So we know that Christ was at least around and available for ministry during Old Testament times.

Now consider how Christ is different from the Father and the Spirit. Of the three persons of the Trinity, the second is the one most involved in manifesting God to man.

We've looked already at Scriptures that tell us no one can see God the Father. Likewise the third person of the Trinity is also associated with an invisible ministry. The Holy Spirit is like the wind, and "the wind blows wherever it pleases. You hear its sound, but you cannot tell where it comes from or where it is going" (John 3:8). Jesus implies that though believers will know the Spirit's indwelling work within them, the Spirit himself will be invisible both to them and to the world, which "neither sees him nor knows him" (John 14:17).

But Scripture emphasizes that the second person of the Trinity is God become flesh, God in human form. He is "Immanuel—which means, 'God with us'" (Matthew 1:23). He's the one and only Son of God who is both "at the Father's side" and *"has made him known"* (John 1:18). "He *appeared* in a body" and "was *seen* by angels" (1 Timothy 3:16).

John describes him with his senses:

> That which was from the beginning, which we have *heard,* which we have *seen* with our eyes, which we have *looked at* and our hands have *touched....* We have *seen* it and testify to it. (1 John 1:1-2)

And someday, "men *will see* the Son of Man coming in clouds with great power and glory" (Mark 13:26).

Christ is God in our sight. Christ is God seeable and touchable and knowable. And the Old Testament ministry of the angel of the Lord is consistent with this. Even the personality of the angel of the Lord seems consistent with what we know of Jesus. Some of the phrases spoken by the angel of the Lord to Gideon remind us of what Christ tells his disciples in the Gospels—"Am I not sending you?" (Judges 6:14). "I will be with you…" (6:16). "Peace! Do not be afraid…" (6:23).

In the last book of the Old Testament—the last book written before the coming of the Christ—the promised Messiah is described as "the Messenger of the covenant, whom you desire" (Malachi 3:1). In Hebrew this word "messenger" is the same term commonly translated as "angel," so the phrase in Malachi is often rendered "the *angel* of the covenant." This title could be a designation that bridges "the angel of the Lord" with Christ, here on the final pages before the old covenant gives way to the new. Jesus could be the "Angel of the Lord" just as surely as he is the "Angel of the Covenant."

Another intriguing passage that may speak to this topic is 1 Corinthians 10:1-4. Paul is recalling the Hebrews who followed Moses out of Egypt. Think back to those days for God's people: We read how "the angel of God" traveled with them in connection with a pillar of cloud and fire (Exodus 14:19). And on Mount Sinai the Lord made this promise to them: "My angel will go ahead of you and bring you into the land" (23:23). Notice what God says about this faithful guide:

> See, I am sending an angel ahead of you to guard you along the way and to bring you to the place I have prepared. Pay attention to him and listen to what he says. Do not rebel against him; *he will not forgive your rebellion, since my Name is in him.* (23:20-21)

This angel is definitely a cut above ordinary angels, for God's very "Name" was in him. Also, he could forgive sins—and 'who can forgive sins but God alone?" (Mark 2:7). The angel of the Lord was personally guiding the Israelites from Egypt to the Promised Land.

Paul now recalls the Hebrews' wilderness experience in spiritual terms:

> They were all baptized into Moses in the cloud and in the sea. They all ate the same spiritual food and drank the same spiritual drink; for they drank from the spiritual rock that accompanied them, and *that rock was Christ.* (1 Corinthians 10:2-4)

The "spiritual rock" that accompanied Israel in the wilderness, Paul says, was Christ. Christ was there!

It could be that late on the first Easter afternoon, when the resurrected Jesus walked unrecognized with Cleopas and his friend on the road from Jerusalem to Emmaus and "explained to them what was said in *all* the Scriptures concerning *himself*"—it just might be he had something to say that afternoon about once making a promise to Hagar beside a desert spring, and once keeping Abraham from killing his son, and once talking to Moses from a burning bush, and once rising up in flames before Manoah and his wife, and even once flashing a sword to a frightened donkey and his unsuspecting rider.

God Was There

But what difference does all this make to us?

First of all, it shows us God's love. In Old Testament times the Scriptures were not yet complete, the Son of God had not yet lived out his sacrificial ministry, and the Holy Spirit's indwelling ministry had not yet given birth to the Church. How privileged we are today to have all these!

But God in his love still provided a special grace to his people through the ministry of the angel of the Lord. God *cared deeply* for them in their condition, and he did something about it. Isaiah puts it well:

In all their distress he too was distressed

and *the angel of his presence saved them.*

In his love and mercy he redeemed them;

he lifted them up and carried them all the days of old. (63:9)

In so many critical moments of Old Testament history, God was there in the form of his angel, providing his loving guidance: when the seed of the nation was begun in the lives of Abraham, Isaac, and Jacob; when the people were led by Moses out of bondage and across the wilderness; and as they faced many trials and enemies in the land God had chosen for them.

Appearances of the angel of the Lord ceased after the birth of Jesus Christ—a further bit of evidence that he may indeed have been that angel. That fact also teaches us the supreme importance of Christ's incarnation, and of the ministry of the Holy Spirit, and of the revelation of Scripture in its entirety. Now that we have those, we do not need the angel of the Lord.

Understand especially that Christ could not have saved us as the angel of the Lord. To accomplish our redemption, he had to become flesh. He had to become *one of us*—not an angel.

> Since the children have flesh and blood, he too shared in their humanity.... For surely it is not angels he helps, but Abraham's descendants. For this reason he had to be made like his brothers in every way...that he might make atonement for the sins of the people. (Hebrews 2:14-17)

It's seems highly possible that in the Old Testament, Christ came to earth in the form of an angel—the greatest Angel. But it's the most absolute, most dependable and undeniable fact in all history that in the New Testament Christ came to earth as a man—the greatest Man, even God himself among us.

Chapter Ten

SHOWING US
HOW TO WORSHIP

I N HIS WISE and warm book *Somewhere Angels,* Larry Libby tells children (and their parents) about two important things in particular we can learn from angels.

One of them is this: "We can learn how to worship the Lord with all our heart."

Angels worship not only wholeheartedly, but also all the time, Libby suggests.

> I think angels have been worshiping from the time they first opened their eyes and saw God's smile....
>
> There are even special angels around God's throne who never, ever stop praising His name. They don't have rest time or recess. They don't go home at night because there is no night—and they wouldn't want to leave God's side even if there was. Shouting and singing praise to the Lord is all they do—and all they *want* to do—forever and ever.

Jesus spoke of angels who "always see the face of my Father in heaven" (Matthew 18:10). I'm sure the result of their unbroken gaze into his face is lots of rich, genuine *worship.*

Wouldn't it be exciting to be a part of that?

Of all the things we've bungled over the years in the Church, worship is maybe the biggest. If giving glory to God is mankind's chief purpose, somehow Satan has gotten us caught up in other agendas. What goes on in lots of places in the name of worship is not really that at all. We've lost the sense of what it means to truly worship God.

The angels can help us rediscover it.

When we first met angelic beings in Scripture, they guarded the gate to the earthly Paradise, keeping Adam and Eve from the tree of life. But several hundred pages later, when we reach the last chapter in Revelation, John actually gets an angel-guided tour of heavenly Paradise, with the tree of life thriving in the middle of it. After the tour the angel says to John, *"Worship God!"*

Between the Garden of Eden in Genesis and the New Jerusalem in Revelation, lots of angelic worship takes place. And the angels' kind of worship is the *real* kind. We have lots to learn from them.

Angels worship so well because they always obey God perfectly, and worship is one of the things he's commanded them to do (and us too). We can actually hear him commanding every single angel to worship his Son Jesus Christ in Hebrews 1:6—

> When God brings his firstborn into the world, he says, *"Let all God's angels worship him."*

Angels live in the presence of God, and stay focused on God, and this is where they get their majesty and awe. With that kind of lifestyle, how could they be anything *but* majestic and awesome? I wonder what you and I would be like if we camped each night beside God's throne in glory, and stayed full of his presence even when we went out into the world to do his work?

I've been around a few people like that. Haven't you? When you're with them you're almost unsure what to say. There's something so different about them. So you reach the same conclusion that was made about the disciples in Acts 4:13—they've "been with Jesus." The Lord is all they seem to want to talk about, and they make you want to think more about him too.

Maybe they've taken lessons from an angel, like the one A. W. Tozer reflects upon:

> If some watcher or holy one who has spent his glad centuries by the sea of fire were to come to earth, how meaningless to him would be the ceaseless chatter of the busy tribes of men.... And were such a one to speak on earth would he not speak of God? Would he not charm and fascinate his hearers with rapturous descriptions of the Godhead? And after hearing him could we ever again consent to listen to anything less than theology, the doctrine of God? Would we not thereafter demand of those who would presume to teach us that they speak to us from the mount of divine vision or remain silent altogether?

As we go to the "mount of divine vision" in Scripture, I think especially of two lessons about worship that angels teach us most: The *fear of God* in worship, and *freedom* in worship.

Fear of God

Remember Psalm 89:7? God's holy angels don't just fear him. They fear him *greatly:*

> In the council of the holy ones God is *greatly feared;*
> he is more awesome than all who surround him.

Here is Scripture using that word *awesome,* which you've seen popping up again and again in this book. It's a shame that through overuse and misuse in our culture this word has lost nearly all the power it once had. With its older meaning, there's really no word quite like it for describing what we encounter so often in this book. *Awesome* means "inspiring awe," and *awe* in turn means "fear mingled with reverence; a feeling produced by something majestic and sublime." Keep that classic meaning in mind as you picture the angels looking around in their "council" in heaven and across the horizon of the universe, and seeing nothing and no one that even remotely approaches the awesomeness of God. They know he's sublimely and majestically holy—awesomely holy. Therefore they show him "fear mingled with reverence."

The richest scenes of heavenly worship in all of Scripture are in Revelation. Here the angelic beings demonstrate their reverence for God, and make a point of doing so again and again. "Day and night" the four living creatures "never stop saying, '*Holy, holy, holy* is the Lord God Almighty'" (4:8). And "whenever" those living creatures offer up that praise, "the twenty-four elders *fall down* before him who sits on the throne, and worship him," and they "*lay their crowns before the throne*" (4:10).

In John's vision, after Christ had taken from God's hands the scroll with seven seals, "the four living creatures and the twenty-four elders *fell down* before the Lamb" (4:8). There were more songs of praise, and then "the four living creatures said, 'Amen,' and the elders *fell down* and worshiped" (4:14).

After six of the seals on the scroll had been opened,

> *All the angels* were standing around the throne and around the elders and the four living creatures. *They fell down on their faces* before the throne and worshiped God…. (7:11)

The opening of the seventh seal brings out seven angels with seven trumpets, and after the last of these has been sounded, "the twenty-four elders, who were seated on their thrones before God, *fell on their faces* and worshiped God…." (11:16).

From all we can tell in Scripture, these spirit beings right now are worshiping in this very manner the same God whom you and I claim as our Lord. If these holy creatures, awesome as they are, cry out in praise of his holiness day and night, how much should we? If they who are pure and splendid fall down before God again and again, how often should we?

Have we had the wrong idea about worship? Are we leaving out too much reverence? Are we trying in vain to get cozier with God, when we should instead be mindful of the distance that must forever stand between us?

M. J. Erickson writes,

> Some worship, rightfully stressing the joy and confidence that the believer has in relationship to a loving heavenly Father, goes beyond that point to an excessive familiarity treating him as an equal, or worse yet, as a servant.... While there are room and need for enthusiasm of expression, and perhaps even an exuberance, that should never lead to a loss of respect. There will always be a sense of awe and wonder.... Although there are love and trust and openness between us and God, we are not equals. He is the almighty, sovereign Lord. We are his servants and followers.

In a sense, fear is simply our honest recognition of the facts. God is holy in and of himself. We are not. And holiness being what it is—exclusive, set apart, untouchable, unknowable, fiery and consuming—we cannot be simply casual and carefree and comfortable around it.

Angels practice the fear of God because they're already in his presence. We must have fear of God because someday we'll be there too, to see God's holiness up close.

We grow in fearing the Lord as we think more clearly about the moment when *we'll* appear before him. When the time comes to receive our rewards, we'll stand wholly accountable to God for the responsibilities he's given us as his children here. Whatever I'm planning right now, or whatever I'm thinking, or whatever I'm doing, or whatever I'm saying will either count for God's kingdom or count for nothing. I'll find out about it all on that day I stand before him.

When Paul said, "Since, then, *we know what it is to fear the Lord*," it was immediately after he had warned us,

For we must all appear before the judgment seat of Christ, *that each one may receive what is due him* for the things done while in the body, whether good or bad. (2 Corinthians 5:10-11)

The standards by which we'll be measured at Christ's judgment seat are the perfect standards of the holy God. Therefore we fear him.

But fear of God is bigger than that. In fact our fear of him will continue even in heaven, even after judgment. In a great scene of worship in Revelation 19, after the twenty-four elders and the four living creatures cry "Hallelujah," a voice comes from heaven's throne to God's redeemed people: "Praise our God, all you his servants, you who *fear him,* both small and great!" This takes place as we're called to the great wedding supper of the Lamb.

Even in eternity we'll still be gratefully redeemed human beings, fearing God with good, perfect fear.

Earlier we looked briefly at Psalm 99, a celebration of the one who "sits enthroned between the cherubim." Three times in this brief song we're reminded of something about God: "he is *holy*" (verse 3); "he is *holy*" (verse 5); "the Lord our God is *holy*" (verse 9). The cherubim understand this truth. We must also understand it, and fear.

"In olden days men of faith were said to 'walk in the fear of God' and to 'serve the Lord with fear,'" A. W. Tozer reminds us. "However intimate their communion with God, however bold their prayers, at the base of their religious life was the conception of God as awesome and dreadful." Why and how have we lost this "healing fear," as Tozer goes on to call it?

We eagerly desire wisdom, and we search for life-knowledge, yet we forget what the Bible gives as the only starting place for it: "The *fear of the Lord* is the beginning of wisdom, and knowledge of the *Holy One* is understanding" (Proverbs 9:10).

In Psalm 36, the first fault David finds with the sinner is that "there is *no fear* of God before his eyes." Perhaps it's also the first fault the angels would find with our worship—and the first fault we should repair, "because of the angels" (1 Corinthians 11:10).

Freedom in Worship

Although angels are so perfect in their fear of God, we don't sense at all that they're *frozen* in fear. Instead they demonstrate great freedom in their worship. They're free to worship God the way he wants to be worshiped.

Reflect again on the Scripture scenes below and this time notice the indications of the angels' energy and movement and emotion in their relationship with God:

In Ezekiel's vision he saw the cherubim moving "wherever the spirit would go" (1:12), and they *"sped back and forth* like flashes of lightning" (1:14).

In Jacob's dream he saw the angels *ascending and descending* on the stairway leading into the Lord's presence (Genesis 28:12). Jesus describes them *"ascending and descending* on the Son of Man" (John 1:51).

In Job 38:7, the heavenly beings sing together and *shout for joy* in recognition of God's work.

In Hebrews 12:22 the myriads of angels are described as being "in *joyful* assembly."

Throughout Revelation we see not only the angels' continual acts of great reverence for God and the Lamb, but also their exuberant outbursts of freely given praise. In 5:8-9 the four living creatures and twenty-four elders all have harps, and John hears them singing "a new song."

One of the most memorable pictures is in Revelation 7. After a great multitude of the redeemed (in white robes and holding palm branches) has praised God, the angels and living creatures and elders have another turn at doing this themselves. We hear their shouts of worship like pealing bells or salutes of cannon-fire:

Amen!
Praise and glory
and wisdom and thanks and honor
and power and strength
be to our God for ever and ever.
Amen! (7:12)

As John stared at this vision, he might have thought it impossible for worship to get any richer and more powerful and triumphant. But the crescendo keeps building.

In chapter 19 there's an overflowing of joy marked by four great shouts of "Hallelujah!" from the "great multitude in heaven." They shout to God, "Let us rejoice and be glad and give him glory!" as the Lamb's wedding supper is announced. They rejoice especially that the Lamb's bride is given "fine linen, bright and clean" to wear. The angels know these wedding clothes represent "the righteous acts of the saints," and they share our joy over them.

It's no wonder that at this point John fell down to worship the angel who was showing him all this.

What a freedom and fullness of joy we see here—and to think it's all because of what God did for *us!* So weren't *we* made to worship this deeply too? If the angels shout "Hallelujah!" on our behalf, surely we can feel free to do it in our own worship as well.

Mature believers know that a heart full of thanksgiving is the most fertile soil for freedom in worship. But offering thanks isn't reserved just for redeemed mankind. We see the twenty-four elders demonstrating this for us in 11:16-17. They fall on their faces and say,

We *give thanks* to you, Lord God Almighty,
the One who is and who was,
because you have taken your great power and have begun to reign.

Just as Psalm 99 promotes fear in worship by reminding us of God's holiness, the next psalm promotes our freedom in worship through thanksgiving. *"Shout for joy to the Lord,"* Psalm 100 begins. We're warmly invited to "worship the Lord with *gladness,"* to "come before him with *joyful songs,"* and to "enter his gates with *thanksgiving."*

Just as God's holiness is the reason for our fear, so God's good and faithful love is the reason for our freedom and thanksgiving. The psalm concludes,

> *Give thanks* to him and praise his name.
> For *the Lord is good* and his *love* endures forever;
> his *faithfulness* continues through all generations.

Soaring in Freedom

The cherubim give us another strong angelic picture of liberated worship.

God gave specific instructions that the sculpted cherubim on the atonement cover of the Ark of the Covenant were "to have their *wings spread upward"* (Exodus 25:20). Centuries later, when the Ark was moved from the tabernacle into Solomon's temple, the wings of the great fifteen-foot-high cherubim in the Holy of Holies were also crafted "with their wings spread out" (1 Kings 6:27). Wings are for flying, and the cherubim's wings gave God's people a picture of free flight in the presence of God.

We can understand why the wings of the cherubim sculptures were designed as they were when we meet the real cherubim through Ezekiel's vision: "Their wings were spread out upward" (Ezekiel 1:11).

Wings are moving parts, and one of the strongest impressions upon Ezekiel in this vision was the loud noise made by their motion. The noise always reminded him of God:

When the creatures moved, I heard *the sound of their wings,* like the
roar of rushing waters, *like the voice of the Almighty,* like the tumult of
an army. (1:24)

The sound of the wings of the cherubim could be heard as far away as
the outer court, *like the voice of God Almighty* when he speaks. (10:5)

The cherubim in God's presence aren't locked into silent stillness, but
are engaged in free and active (and noisy!) worship.

Perhaps the six-winged seraphim in Isaiah 6 show something of the
same picture. Isaiah says that with two of their wings "they were flying," and
their flight may be as much an expression of free worship as of carrying out
their work.

In his commentary on this passage, Matthew Henry asks us,

If angels come upon the wing from heaven to earth to minister for
our good, shall not we soar upon the wing from earth to heaven, to
share with them in their glory?

We too "will soar on wings like eagles" (Isaiah 40:31) as we hope in the
Lord and let his strength renew us. Our soaring can take place as much in
worship as anywhere else, when our hearts and hands and voices rise freely
above personal and cultural inhibitions.

God's sovereign rule for us now is the "perfect law that gives freedom"
(James 1:25), and in that freedom we must have the liberty to "lift up our
hearts and our hands to God in heaven" (Lamentations 3:41). For "where
the Spirit of the Lord is, there is freedom" (2 Corinthians 3:17).

Summon the Angels to Worship

So the angels help us worship. Can *we* help the angels worship?

Maybe we can!

Occasionally in the Psalms, the human writer invokes praise for God
from the angels. David does it in Psalm 29 and 103—

Ascribe to the Lord, *O mighty ones,*
>   ascribe to the Lord glory and strength.
Ascribe to the Lord the glory due his name;
>   *worship the Lord* in the splendor of his holiness. (29:1-2)

Praise the Lord, you his angels,
>   you mighty ones who do his bidding,
>   who obey his word.
Praise the Lord, all his heavenly hosts,
>   you his servants who do his will. (103:20-21)

The unknown author of Psalm 148 makes the same request:

Praise the Lord from the heavens,
>   praise him in the heights above.
Praise him, all his angels,
>   *praise him, all his heavenly hosts.* (148:1-2)

Would the angels really listen to a mere man asking them to praise God?

Why not? As Larry Libby says in *Somewhere Angels,* "They'll praise the Lord for any reason at all, and love doing it."

Maybe God has worked out something special with them in advance. Knowing how thrilling and fulfilling worship is for angels, maybe he's told them, "As I work in the hearts of my people on earth, and they call out the Scriptures that summon you to praise me, I'll gladly allow you the privilege of responding to their words. You can take their cue to make your songs to me even sweeter and your shouts even louder!"

It's probably worth a try. Go ahead and look up sometime, and ask the angels to pour on the coals in their worship intensity. But make sure you're doing the same to yours.

Fire and Wind Again

To get the most from the angels for our worship, we can go back once more to fire and wind, the apt imagery for angels that God gives us in Psalm 104 and Hebrews 1.

In our worship, the fire reminds us of fear. Like the angels, we fear God, for our God is a consuming fire. His blazing holiness leads us onward into accountability and fear.

Likewise in our worship, the wind reminds us of freedom and the Spirit. Like the angels we want to be free as the wind, as bold as a breeze in Spirit-directed worship. For "the wind blows wherever it pleases," and "so it is with everyone born of the Spirit" (John 3:8). God's soaring love leads us onward into thanksgiving and freedom.

To stay balanced in your worship and devotion to God, saturate your heart with both aspects: Fear and freedom. Fire and wind. God's great holiness and God's great love.

Tomorrow, as you meet with the Lord of the morning for your personal and private devotion, lock into both sides of worship.

And remember both sides as well next Sunday when you meet with the family of God. You can't cause others there to dive deeper into worship, but you can be responsible for your own heart, and have it ready to meet God more fully in public, corporate worship than you ever have before.

And that, in turn, will make you better fitted for the day up there when we unite in perfect praise with the angels.

Chapter Eleven

SHOWING US
HOW TO WORK

ANOTHER GOOD lesson we can pick up from angels, according to Larry Libby in his children's book *Somewhere Angels,* is this: "We learn the great joy of obeying God quickly."

Calvin reflects that "in accommodation to us," Scripture has shown us the wings of seraphim and cherubim "to assure us that when occasion requires they will hasten to our aid with incredible swiftness, winging their way to us with the speed of lightning."

Once more the fire and wind illustration suggest a potent picture: The angels in their obedient service are as intense as flames, and as quick as the wind. Angels are just as good at the *work* God gives them as they are at *worship.*

God can count on them, and so can we. There's no sloppy workmanship or laziness or negligence on their part.

When David summons the angels to praise God in Psalm 103, he calls them "you mighty ones who *do his bidding,* who *obey his word…* you his servants who *do his will.*"

Angels get so absorbed in their work that even their appearance is governed by their assignment. Depending on the task God gives them in serving us, they may remain invisible to our eyes, or appear in ordinary human form, or take on some more glorious aspect. Their form—what they *are*—

depends on their function—what they *do.* As J. M. Wilson says, "In general they are simply regarded as *embodiments of their mission.*"

Here again let's recall Hebrews 1:14. It's a rich verse, and we can draw truth and implications and reflections about angelic work from every phrase: (a) the angels are *sent forth* (they're on assignment); (b) they're sent forth *to minister* (that means *service,* and service means *work); (c) all* angels are thus sent forth (no loafers among them); and (d) they go only *to those who will inherit salvation* (their labor benefits us!).

With David's words in Psalm 34:7 in mind—"The angel of the Lord encamps around those who fear him"—Matthew Henry comments on several aspects of angelic work. He notes that God uses angels

> for the protection of his people from the malice and power of evil spirits; and the holy angels do us more good offices every day than we are aware of.
>
> Though in dignity and in capacity of nature they are very much superior to us … though they have constant employment in the upper world, the employment of praising God, and are entitled to a constant rest and bliss there—yet in obedience to their Maker, and in love to those that bear his image, they condescend to minister to the saints, and stand up for them against the powers of darkness; they not only visit them, but encamp round about them, acting for their good….

Angels get different instructions for different people in different circumstances. The angels appearing to Daniel told him to "seal up" the vision and prophetic words he'd been given (Daniel 8:26, 12:4), because "it concerns the distant future." (By the way, scholars think this may be why Daniel's visions are recorded in his own Hebrew tongue, while the rest of Daniel is written in Aramaic, the most common language of the Babylonian Empire.) But in Revelation, the angel speaking with John specifically told him, "Do *not* seal up the words of the prophecy of this book, because the

SHOWING US HOW TO WORK   183

time is near" (22:10). No doubt angels have to be careful to follow their instructions exactly.

As we noted earlier, the word *angel* means "messenger," so messenger-work appears to be a big part of an angel's job description. And angels are *trustworthy* messengers. In Luke 2 the shepherds went into Bethlehem to see the baby Jesus, and they found everything "just as they had been told" (2:20). Who had given the shepherds such an accurate picture of what to expect? It was an angel.

When the angel tells John in Revelation, "These are the *true words* of God" (19:9), and "These words are *trustworthy* and *true*" (22:6), we don't doubt it for a minute. Angels tell the truth.

We looked before at how these truth-telling messengers were especially involved in communicating God's law to mankind, which was "put into effect through angels" (Galatians 3:19, Acts 7:53). As holy beings who have always obeyed God perfectly, the angels probably have total comprehension of God's law for mankind. They know it and understand it better than you and I do the alphabet. The Bible never says angels desire to know more about the law; what they "long to look into" is the matter of our salvation (1 Peter 1:12), our redemption as those whom the law condemns but whom Jesus died for. Since we as human beings didn't live up to the law the angels brought to us, I'm sure they were thrilled out of their wings to also be assigned messenger-duty in communicating the coming of our Savior, who saves us from the law's curse.

Another angelic service to us is shown in Revelation 7:3-4. Angels put a seal "on the foreheads of the servants of our God," and this seal marks believers as belonging to the Lord. It's in contrast to the "mark of the beast" worn by those who belong to the devil (13:16-17), and who thus are destined to receive God's tormenting wrath (14:9-11). We can be thankful that the angels will be accurate and thorough in this service. (Wouldn't you hate to be a believer whom the angels inadvertently forgot to seal that day?)

As we've seen many times, everything good or noble or noteworthy about angels is directly attributable to something good or noble or noteworthy about God. Their faithfulness in their work is no exception.

The angels are faithful at work because they see the faithfulness of God in *his* work. A man in the Bible named Ethan knew this for sure. "Who's Ethan?" you may be saying. He isn't as well known as Daniel or John or Ezekiel, but perhaps of all human beings who have walked the earth, none had greater insight into angels than Ethan—Daniel and John and Ezekiel being the only exceptions, by virtue of their stunning visions.

Ethan the Ezrahite was noted for his wisdom (1 Kings 4:31) in the days of Solomon. He's likely the same Ethan who was originally appointed by Solomon's father David as one of the leaders among the temple musicians (1 Chronicles 15:19). Part of his job in the celebrations at the house of the Lord was "to sound the bronze cymbals."

He also was the writer of the 89th Psalm. We quoted it earlier. It's the one that mentions how God is "greatly feared" in "the council of the holy ones." Ethan also specifically says that God's *"faithfulness* too" is praised "in the assembly of the holy ones." And after citing the angelic praise for this faithfulness, Ethan adds his own:

> O Lord God of Hosts, who is like you?
>   You are mighty, O Lord,
>   and your *faithfulness* surrounds you. (89:8)

Ethan knew that angels are faithful to us because God is faithful to us.

Throughout this book we've seen plenty of examples of the angels at work—from defending Eden to feeding Elijah, and healing Isaiah's sinful lips, and springing Peter out of jail, and showing John around New Jerusalem, and lots more. Now that we've highlighted so much of their labor, some particular questions about it are worth delving into.

Do I Have My Own Guardian Angel?

Is there one particular angel whose God-given assignment is serving me—just *me?*

There are plenty of folks who think that. Guardian angels are mainstream America these days. "GET IN TOUCH WITH YOUR OWN GUARDIAN ANGEL!" screamed a recent full-page advertisement in a leading magazine.

Many years ago, before I was ordained to the gospel ministry, I had to go through an ordination council in Haddon Heights, New Jersey. As a pastor, my father was on the ordination committee. My mother had also been invited to be in the room and watch the proceedings.

The committee reviewed a paper in which I outlined my doctrinal beliefs, then called me up for questioning on all the different levels and aspects of theology. When they came to the subject of angels, one of the committee members asked me, "David, do you believe in guardian angels?"

Before I could answer, my mother (I couldn't believe she did this) raised her voice and said, "Well if he doesn't, I do."

When she heard that question, who knows how many close calls during my growing-up years came flashing into her mind?

One of them I still remember as vividly as if it happened yesterday, though it occurred more than forty years ago.

My uncle had a farm near Binghamton, New York where I visited in the summertime. I was a city boy and didn't know much about a farm, but I learned a lot from my uncle.

One summer I was intrigued by the silos that towered up beside the barn. There were two of them. At that time one was full nearly to the top with silage, and the other was still empty, waiting to be filled.

I got the idea I wanted to climb up the outside of the silo that was full. I would slip through the little metal door at the top and land on the silage. Up there I could be in my own little world for a while.

So I climbed the ladder that scaled the outside. I don't know their exact dimensions, but man, those silos are *high*. As you go up you feel you're just hanging out in the middle of nowhere. I was stepping real slow, trying to be careful.

At the top I opened the door and swung my foot into the darkness. Just as I leaned in, I looked down and realized an awful fact: I had climbed the wrong silo! The one I was about to fall into was empty. There was nothing there—all the way to the ground.

I think that's the closest I ever came to not being here to write this book for you. I hung on with both hands and slowly eased myself back out to the ladder. Shaking like a leaf, I climbed down.

I've always believed that an angel saved me up there. That's one of the encounters that comes to my mind when I'm asked if I believe in guardian angels. Anyway, my mother believes in them.

What does the Bible say about them?

Psalm 91:11-12 gives a general overview of the angels providing protection for God's people:

> For he will command his *angels* concerning you
> > to guard you in all your ways;
> they will lift you up in their hands,
> > so that you will not strike your foot against a stone.

But that verse speaks of angels, plural. What about the concept of *one* particular angel assigned only to me?

Many theologians over the centuries have believed this way, including Thomas Aquinas, who thought everyone has a guardian angel assigned to him at birth. But what does the Bible say?

Two passages are pointed to most often in discussing the question of guardian angels. In the first, Jesus tells his disciples,

> See that you do not look down on one of these little ones. For I tell
> you that *their angels* in heaven always see the face of my Father in
> heaven. (Matthew 18:10)

From these words some would assert that a number of God's angels are
assigned to stand ready before the Father to respond instantly to his command for protection and care over these "little ones." Jesus calls them *"their
angels."* But others would point out that the passage doesn't say these angels
do any "guarding" of the "little ones"—in fact, they apparently "always" stay
in God's presence. Nor does the passage specifically match one angel to each
"little one."

The second passage that supporters of the guardian angel concept point
to is Acts 12, where Peter is miraculously delivered from prison. It's one of
everyone's favorite Bible stories. When we retold it earlier, we left Peter
standing in the middle of the street. The angel had awakened him in his
prison cell, ordered him to get dressed, slipped him out past guards and
through gates, then led him out into the cool night air of freedom. Now the
angel disappeared. Peter "came to himself." No longer groggy, he acknowl-
edged what the Lord's angel had done, then went to a house where some of
the believers had gathered and were praying.

The scene awaiting him there "was one of confusion and joyful humor,"
as one commentator describes it, and "must have led to hilarity every time
it was repeated among the early believers."

> Peter knocked at the outer entrance, and a servant girl named Rhoda
> came to answer the door. When she recognized Peter's voice, she was
> so overjoyed she ran back without opening it and exclaimed, "Peter
> is at the door!"
>
> "You're out of your mind," they told her. When she kept insisting
> that it was so, they said, *"It must be his angel."*
>
> But Peter kept on knocking, and when they opened the door and
> saw him, they were astonished. (12:13-16)

The believers praying for Peter thought it was "his angel" that the flustered servant girl had encountered at the door. Surely, some would say, they were referring to his guardian angel. But Rhoda had only heard a voice at the door. Why would Peter's guardian angel have a voice that sounded like Peter's? What the believers really were thinking, some say, is that Peter had been killed, and "his angel" was their way of referring to his disembodied spirit. No wonder they were hesitant to open the door.

Besides these passages, there's no other obvious scriptural evidence for *individual* guardian angels, so the case for them isn't a strong one.

But if this is disappointing news to you, and you're dismayed to think there may not be a specific angel responsible for your protection, you need not jump up in fear to check the locks on your doors and windows. There's plenty of evidence that God himself is looking out for you, in addition to all the angels he chooses to use in carrying out the job.

I love John Calvin's thoughts on this:

> Whether or not each believer has a single angel assigned to him for his defense, I dare not positively affirm....
>
> This, indeed, I hold for certain, that each of us is cared for *not by one angel merely,* but that all with one consent watch for our safety.

"After all," he adds,

> it is not worthwhile anxiously to investigate a point which does not greatly concern us. If anyone does not think it enough to know that all the orders of the heavenly host are perpetually watching for his safety, I do not see what he could gain by knowing that he has one angel as a special guardian.

One thing we know for sure: Our God uses his awesome power in a compassionate, loving way to help those who need help. I like that about God. I've felt His love and compassion in many ways in recent months, and I know he's that kind of God. While on the one hand he's holy, there's the other side of it too: He condescends to be concerned about such as us, and will even dispatch one angel or an army of them for our service and protection.

There's great hope in that.

This is a good time to remind ourselves again that angels are created beings—*God's* created beings. He's told us much about them, but he's also withheld much. Even if he told us everything, however—even if we knew all there is to know about angels—the simple truth still would stand that they belong to God. They're his, and he can do with them whatever he wills. They aren't ours to control or to use. They aren't ours to satisfy either our physical and emotional needs or our intellectual curiosity.

They serve us, but they are not our servants. God alone is their Master. When they minister to us, it's because God has so directed, and not because we have commanded or even requested their service.

Are Angels Still Involved in Warfare?

Now back for a moment to the military aspect of angels. There's no way around it: A big part of angel work is warfare.

The angels are warriors because God is. "*The Lord is a warrior;* the Lord is his name" (Exodus 15:3). David, the man after God's own heart, tells us in song that God "expresses his wrath *every day*" (Psalm 7:11).

Here's a picture David gives of God getting ready for this daily work:

> He will sharpen his sword;
>> he will bend and string his bow.
> He has prepared his deadly weapons;
>> he makes ready his flaming arrows. (7:12-13)

Psalm 78 shows God on the warpath in his plagues against Pharaoh. This psalm by Asaph recounts the rivers of blood and the swarms of flies and frogs, the pestilence of grasshopper and locust, and the storms of hail and sleet and lightning bolts that devastated the Egyptians. The Lord "unleashed against them *his hot anger, his wrath, indignation and hostility*" (78:49).

In the same verse Asaph tells us who God used for this angry work: "a band of *destroying angels.*"

But God the Divine Warrior isn't only an Old Testament concept. Look again at the picture of Christ that was revealed first to John, and through him to us:

> There before me was a white horse, whose rider is called Faithful and True. With justice he judges and makes war.... Out of his mouth comes a sharp sword with which to strike down the nations.... He treads the winepress of the fury of the wrath of God Almighty. (Revelation 19:11-15)

And look again at who is with Christ in this scene:

> The *armies of heaven* were following him, riding on white horses.... (19:14)

Yes, God is a warrior and he wins every battle. Because of that, the angels also never lose.

If this thought of a Warrior God and warrior angels is disturbing—if you'd rather think of peace—then remember that your peace is possible only because of powerful protection (both by angels and through the Holy Spirit) that shields you from Satan and his wicked hosts. Battle is being waged on your behalf. If it wasn't, just how long do you think you could withstand the devil's attacks, fighting alone? Could you hold out even half a minute? And once you were conquered, as you inevitably would be, how much mercy could you honestly expect from this enemy, considering his character and background?

Thank God he is a Warrior!

Does God Do All His Work through Angels?

In a letter addressed to God, a little girl wrote,

> Dear God,
>
> Do you get your angels to do all your work? Mommy says that we are *her* angels and we have to do everything.

I think God's answer would be that no, he doesn't get angels to do *all* his work. (And they won't do all of ours, either.)

God *could* do everything himself, without ever using angels or nature or Christians or anything else. Or God can use those agents to accomplish whatever he wants, without in any way limiting his sovereignty. As M. J. Erickson reminds us, "God is not limited to working directly to accomplish his purposes."

God always does what he wants to do, and he does it the way he wants. He may use an angel to do some service one moment—a word of encouragement to a stranger perhaps, or locating a lost item for someone, or providing a needed gift of finances or food—and the next moment use a Christian to do an identical deed—and the next moment accomplish the same purposes by using neither angel nor man.

Therefore if God the Almighty can indeed send angels—or anything else—to our aid, then let's never stop praying for his help. Remember that the angel Gabriel came to Daniel specifically in response to his prayer (9:23), though Daniel was *not* praying to see or be served by an angel.

If I Sense an Angel's Presence, How Can I Be Sure?

When Gabriel appeared to Daniel, he told him, "Therefore *consider* the message, and *understand* the revelation." Daniel saw the angel and heard him, but Daniel was still required to put his own mental energy into evaluating all that the angel communicated to him.

This could well be God's command to us about angels as well— first in regard to what his Scripture says about them, and second in regard to our own experience.

"*Consider*...and *understand*...." How much are you doing that even now, as you study this topic? Are you really putting your mind to work as you look over the scriptural record?

"*Consider*...and *understand*...." How much are you prepared to do this as well if you encounter the presence of a totally spiritual being?

The Bible is clear: We are to "test the spirits" (1 John 4:1-3)—and angels are spirits. Paul said it too: "Test everything. Hold on to the good. Avoid every kind of evil" (1 Thessalonians 5:21-22).

Your best test is to keep Jesus Christ before the eyes of your heart:

> Every spirit that acknowledges that Jesus Christ has come in the flesh is from God, but every spirit that does not acknowledge Jesus is not from God. This is the spirit of the antichrist, which you have heard is coming and even now is already in the world. (1 John 4:2-3)

And suppose an angel did appear to you with some message from God. What would you honestly be more excited about—God's message, or getting to see an angel?

Again and again in the Scriptures we see this pattern: Those who are given the privilege of a direct visible or audible ministry from angels are those with mature hearts who want to encounter God—not angels.

The gospel accounts of the resurrection are a good example. The women and the disciples believed the angelic report of the good news of Jesus' resurrection, but not once did any of them turn their attention and their focus upon the angels. No one got excited about seeing angels. They were excited about what the angels *said.*

Notice what Mary did in John 20:10-18. She carried on a fairly calm conversation with two angels dressed in white, then turned away from them to converse with someone she thought was nothing more than a gardener.

It turned out to be Jesus himself. When she returned to tell the disciples, she didn't say, "I've seen angels," but, "I have seen the Lord." Her heart was right, and therefore God was able to let her see angels.

As a side-note on the angels' work, let's take up a couple of perplexing questions that often arise because of two unusual passages in Scripture.

Do God's Angels Ever Deceive Us?

We noted before how King Ahab died in his bloody chariot on the battle-field after failing to heed the angelic vision recounted to him by the prophet Micaiah. The prophet told Ahab he had seen the Lord "sitting on his throne with all the host of heaven standing on his right and on his left" (1 Kings 22:19, 2 Chronicles 18:18), and that these angels and God were discussing the disaster and death that would soon come to Ahab if he went into battle against Syria. What we didn't mention before is that four hundred other prophets around Ahab didn't agree with Micaiah's outlook. These other prophets told Ahab he *should* go into battle because he was sure to be victorious.

Micaiah told Ahab that these other prophets were liars. Furthermore, he said that their lies had been allowed in the sovereignty of God, and even influenced by one of the spiritual beings conversing around God's throne. Did God actually tell an angel to bring about such deceit?

This time let's listen in on that heavenly conversation as Micaiah relates it to Ahab:

> And the Lord said, "Who will entice Ahab king of Israel into attacking Ramoth Gilead and going to his death there?"
>
> One suggested this, and another that. Finally, *a spirit* came forward, stood before the Lord and said, "I will entice him."
>
> "By what means?" the Lord asked.
>
> "I will go and be *a lying spirit* in the mouths of all his prophets," he said.

"You will succeed in enticing him," said the Lord. "Go and do it."
(1 Kings 22:20-22, 2 Chronicles 18:19-21).

"So now," Micaiah tells Ahab, "the Lord has put *a lying spirit* in the
mouths of these prophets of yours. The Lord has decreed disaster for you."

We might ask, how could an angel stoop to such a trick? And how
could God be a part of it? Wasn't this unfair to Ahab, tyrant and idolater
though he was? And are angels pulling this kind of stunt all the time?

But before jumping to any uncomfortable conclusions, remember first
of all that Ahab is told *everything*—and he finds out all this *before* he goes
into battle, not afterward, when it would be too late to do anything about it.
When Ahab died in his blood-soaked chariot at sunset, he was not the
victim of an angelic deception, but the victim of his own foolishness in not
heeding what God revealed to him. In fact, the shocking vision from heaven
might well have been God's merciful way of using every available means to
grab Ahab's attention and try to turn him around. God held nothing back
from him. However, only Ahab could choose his response. And Ahab chose
wrongly.

We know that God himself is perfectly good, truthful, and holy. Repeat-
edly in Scripture we hear that he hates evil in every form (Psalm 11:5;
Proverbs 6:16-19, 17:15; Isaiah 61:8; Jeremiah 44:2-4; Zechariah 8:17; Malachi 2:16). God's character is affirmed in a prayer of the prophet Habakkuk:
"Your eyes are too pure to look on evil; *you cannot tolerate wrong*" (1:13).

It's possible that the "lying spirit" sent to the four hundred prophets was
a demon or the devil, in a situation similar to the time when Satan appeared
before God and asked for permission to afflict Job. But regardless of the
identity of the spirit Micaiah described, we know that nothing God was
responsible for in Ahab's life could have been evil, nor were his angels
responsible for any evil in that situation. And since God never changes, he
and his servants the angels can never be responsible for evil in our lives
either.

Did the Angels Intermarry with Mankind?

This second perplexing question springs from Genesis 6. Just before we begin the story of God's mercy in saving Noah from the flood, we read this:

> When men began to increase in number on the earth and daughters were born to them, *the sons of God* saw that the daughters of men were beautiful, and they married any of them they chose.… in those days—and also afterward—when *the sons of God* went to the daughters of men and had children by them. (6:1-4)

Who were these "sons of God"? Since the Hebrew term here is used to refer to angels in the opening chapters of Job, some have thought that the Genesis passage is an instance of angels—perhaps even fallen angels—marrying human beings. Jesus' statement that the angels in heaven do not marry (Matthew 22:30, Mark 12:25) may rule out that interpretation.

Another suggested interpretation is that "the sons of God" here represent the more godly descendants of Adam (through his son Seth) who intermarried with those from the more sinful family line of Cain. Another possible understanding is that in Genesis 6 we see simply a poetic way of referring back to how mankind was first created. From the dust of the ground God formed Adam (a "son of God"), while God took a rib from the man to form Eve (a "daughter of man"). So in Genesis 6, when the "sons of God" marry the "daughters of men," it may simply mean that men are marrying women.

More Work Ahead

Angels exist for a reason, a purpose: God made them servants. They have work to do, and they always will. The fact that so many angels exist—and exist for all eternity—helps point us to the picture that our eternal heaven is a very busy place, a dynamic, energetic scene with lots of action, with God himself setting the pace.

When the writer of Hebrews points us toward eternity as if we were already there, he says, "You have come...to the heavenly Jerusalem, the city of the *living* God" (12:22). God is *alive* there—he's not a wax figure in a museum or an elderly grandfather wasting away in a rest home. He's going strong, and heaven is run *his* way, and the angels know it. That's why they stay so busy.

When we get there, I suppose we wouldn't even be able to keep up with angels if it weren't for the fact that we're getting new, spiritual bodies and capacities like theirs.

We have lots of exciting, fulfilling work waiting for us on the other side. So for now, let's learn all we can from the crew already on duty there—our faithful friends, the angels—and let's put it into practice right here.

Chapter Twelve

COMING TO CARRY ME HOME

PEOPLE DIE. For forty years now I've ministered to those who were dying. I've been with them in the process, and I've been in the room after death has occurred. I've watched their loved ones mourn over their loss, trying to hold on to a body where there was no longer any life.

But over time I've learned more about what actually happens in the process between seeing these people holding on to life one minute, then seeing them with no life at all the next.

I've come to believe from Scripture that angels take believers home to heaven when we die. I have to tell you honestly that it took a while before I became really convinced of that. I had always wondered about it. But now I realize there's strong justification for believing it.

I once preached the message of this chapter at the funeral of the mother of someone on our ministry staff. Mrs. Huntsman was ninety-five years old, and was survived by her husband.

During the service I spoke about what happens when a believer dies, and how the angels come to get that person.

After the service, I walked down to greet and comfort Mr. Huntsman, and to tell him I would be praying for him. As I leaned over and spoke to him, he answered so loudly you could hear him all over the chapel (apparently he had turned down his hearing aid). "Oh, Pastor Jeremiah," he said, "it's the part about the angels I love. I just love that about the angels coming to get Gladys."

I was glad it was a comfort to him, and I wish I'd understood it earlier and been able to offer it to others. The loss of a friend or family member can be the deepest darkness known to God's people on earth. In pain the psalmist cried out to God, "You have taken my companions and loved ones from me; the darkness is my closest friend" (Psalm 88:18). But the Scriptures offer hope for us in those dark times.

Before we look closer at what the angels have to do with our death, let's look at death itself.

What Is Death?

The word *death* means "separation." In the New Testament it's the Greek word *thanatos.* Physical death is the separation of the spirit and soul from the body. We'll be more like the angels then, because we'll have lost the part of us that angels don't possess—our physical bodies. After death we no longer exist in both the physical and spiritual realms, but in the spiritual realm alone.

After a person dies his body is only a corpse—"the body without the spirit is dead" (James 2:26). The person's body will only decay, but his spirit and soul will go to be either forever with God or eternally apart from him.

God places great value on the death of the believer. "*Precious* in the sight of the Lord is the death of his saints" (Psalm 116:15). John in his vision heard heaven itself pronouncing this preciousness:

> Then I heard a voice from heaven say, "Write: *Blessed* are the dead who die in the Lord from now on."
>
> "Yes," says the Spirit, "they will rest from their labor, for their deeds will follow them." (Revelation 14:13)

"To die is *gain,*" Paul said (Philippians 1:21).

Christians who grow in their relationship with God understand this blessedness of death. As a Dallas Seminary student I started my ministry career working as an intern chaplain at Baylor Hospital. I often went with the head chaplain to the family room to help someone deal with death. A few times I had to go by myself, when I was on duty alone. I got to the point where I could walk in the room where the family was and within two or three minutes know if I was dealing with Christians or non-Christians. It was uncanny. Death for a believer is difficult and challenging and nothing anybody wants to deal with. It's hard and scary and painful. But it's not despair. It isn't the end.

Not long after I battled cancer, a 34-year-old man in our church died of that disease, and I preached his funeral. I must confess it was a lot harder for me to do that after having had cancer myself.

The cancer had ravished his body in a short period of time. Before he died I visited him at his home. His wife was there, as well as his young son. We sat together in their living room. He talked about going to heaven just as if it he were going to the grocery store. It overwhelmed me. He was telling his little boy, "And when I get there, this is what it's going to be like. I know I'll miss you a lot, but just think what Daddy's going to get to do!"

I had never seen anything quite like it before. It was another indication to me that Christians die differently. There's no question about it. The way believers face death is one of the strongest evidences of the reality of our faith.

Angels for Our Final Journey

So where do angels enter in? Scripture gives us comforting precedence for their special service to us at the time of our death.

Our Lord told a fascinating story in Luke 16 of two men who were as different as they could be. Jesus began their story in such a way as to make the most of the contrast:

There was a rich man who was dressed in purple and fine linen and lived in luxury every day.

At his gate was laid a beggar named Lazarus, covered with sores and longing to eat what fell from the rich man's table. Even the dogs came and licked his sores.

The time came when the beggar died and the angels carried him to Abraham's side.

The rich man also died and was buried. In hell…he was in torment….

Only a gate separated these two men. Lazarus begged on the outside, the rich man lived lavishly on the inside. But Lazarus knew God, and the rich man didn't.

Notice especially the contrast in what happened after their deaths. The rich man "died and was buried." Period. Next we see him in hell.

But when Lazarus died, *"the angels* carried him to Abraham's side." ("Abraham's side" was a picture in the Jewish mind of the feasting and joy we'll know in eternity.) In his lifetime the beggar had licking dogs as his companions, but at his death the angels were honored to convey him into heaven. And they weren't just *with* him; they *"carried* him."

Lazarus was regarded as one of the most inferior of persons in this life, but that didn't disqualify him from having an angel escort through eternity's doorway. Lowly Lazarus was awarded this privilege, and apparently so was the highest of men — the Son of Man himself.

Scripture hints that Jesus may have been carried by angels into heaven on the day of his ascension. In Mark 16:19 we read that "he was *taken up* into heaven." Luke writes that while Jesus was "blessing" his disciples, he left them and was *taken up* into heaven" (24:51). Based on a respected alternative rendering in the Greek text, the King James Version translates the sentence this way: "While he blessed them, he was parted from them, and *carried up* into heaven." In Acts 1:9 we read, "After he said this, he was *taken up* before their very eyes...." Angels may have had this privilege of taking or carrying Jesus up on his return trip home.

Why would angels come to provide this service to us at the time of our deaths?

One reason may be related to the fact that Satan is described as "the ruler of the kingdom of the air" (Ephesians 2:2). Perhaps we must cross this "kingdom of the air" in going from earth to heaven. Our temporary home here and our permanent home there may be separated by an immense stretch of enemy territory. It's a trip angels must take often, so it will be a great comfort to have them at our side as we traverse it ourselves.

In *Somewhere Angels,* Larry Libby gives children another reason:

> God wants you home so much he'll send his own angel to meet you.
> And don't be surprised if the angel is wearing a big smile.

Chapter Thirteen

HELL'S ANGELS

YOU'VE DONE an opposites quiz before, haven't you? I say "small," and if you're sound in mind (at least for the moment) you're supposed to quickly answer "large." I say the word *darkness*, you answer, *light*. I say *soft*, you respond with *hard*. I say *good*, you say *bad*.

And what if I say... "God"?

If you answer "Satan," you're wrong (misinformed maybe, or perhaps a little unsound of mind today).

Satan is not the opposite of God. Satan can't be God's opposite because Satan himself was created by God. Nobody is God's counterpart. But isn't it interesting how Satan has deceived us into believing he is God's equal in power and significance?

We're going to do now what I promised you many pages back—we're going to put our focus for a while on the fallen angels: Satan and the demons who follow him.

When I preached a sermon series on angels in our church, the messages on the devil and his fallen angels drew the biggest response. I never would have dreamed that. I thought those would be sort of parentheses sermons, dealing with necessary negative factors just to get them out of the way so we could focus on positive things about angels. But there was more interest in this than in anything else we covered.

So I know you're curious to learn more on this subject, for it's always good strategy to know your enemy. "We are not unaware of his schemes" (2 Corinthians 2:11), Paul says; therefore he was able to make plans "in order that Satan might not outwit us." We don't want to be unaware of his plots and maneuvers, though in this book we can only hit the highlights.

On the other hand, we want to avoid the preoccupation with the devil that seems to grip some people. Satan is not a center of attention in my life, and I don't think he should be for any Christian. Not that we should disregard him or take him for granted, but you can't focus on two things at the same time. If I'm always worried about Satan, I won't have time to worship God. As Amy Carmichael used to say, "I sing the doxology, and say goodbye to Satan."

I hope the richness of what we've already studied about angels will help you see this topic in perspective. Satan and the fallen angels who follow him were created to partake of the same splendid privileges we've seen the good angels enjoy. All that glorious existence should have been Satan's to delight in as well. How profoundly true is our judgment of his chosen course: "How you have fallen...!" (Isaiah 14:12).

Bible teachers point particularly to two Old Testament passages suggesting the story of Satan's downfall. In Ezekiel 28 we especially find indications of Satan's original state leading up to his fall, while Isaiah 14 seems to focus on Satan's inward rebellion that caused it.

Both of these passages have direct application to earthly rulers other than Satan: Ezekiel is writing "a lament concerning *the king of Tyre*" (28:12), while Isaiah introduces his words as a "taunt against *the king of Babylon*." But the allusions to Satan in each one are strong, giving both passages a more profound bearing.

Here's a good way of looking at these passages: They point *both* to the earthly kings mentioned *and* to Satan, in the same way that some of the messianic passages point both to the Davidic kings of Israel and to Christ. They find their fulfillment on more than one level.

Satan Before

Before we look at the pictures these two prophets paint, let's begin with a key statement by Jesus. He told the Jews that Satan "was a murderer *from the beginning, not holding to the truth*" (John 8:44). Here we see that Satan's fallen state goes back at least before our known human history. This is echoed in 1 John 3:8, where we read that "the devil has been sinning *from the beginning.*"

But the phrase "not holding to the truth" in John 8:44 seems to imply that Satan *could* have held to the truth but didn't, or that he *once did,* but no longer does.

Now on to Ezekiel 28, a passage rich with mystery. In the opening verses of this chapter Ezekiel pronounces judgment against the king of Tyre. But after verse eleven, the prophet's descriptions are difficult if not impossible to ascribe to any human being. Instead he seems to move beyond the human ruler of Tyre and to speak about the true power behind the throne, the "king" who is none other than Satan.

Ezekiel is quoting a description given to him by "the Sovereign Lord" (28:12). He is not describing what he, the prophet, has seen, but what God himself has told him.

The passage is addressed directly to this "king of Tyre." The first several verses mirror his past to him. They go on to remind him that he was once "anointed as a *guardian cherub,*" God says, "for so I ordained you" (28:14).

This guardian cherub was perfect. "You were *the model of perfection,* full of wisdom and perfect in beauty" (28:12). He was perfect in intellect and perfect in form.

The guardian cherub had no light of his own, but from the start he was fully arrayed by his Creator to reflect God's glory:

> *Every precious stone* adorned you:
> ruby, topaz and emerald,
> chrysolite, onyx and jasper,

sapphire, turquoise and beryl.

Your settings and mountings were *made of gold*;
> on the day you were created they were prepared. (28:13)

We also discover *where* God placed this guardian cherub:

You were in *Eden,*
> *the garden of God....*
You were on the *holy mount of God;*
> you walked among the fiery stones. (28:13-14)

Satan After

In the next verse we return to the theme of the cherub's perfection—and
suddenly we watch that perfection come crashing down.

You were blameless in your ways
> from the day you were created
> till *wickedness was found in you.* (28:15)

The next verses spell out that wickedness, accusing the guardian cherub
of violence and especially pride, leading to his expulsion from God's presence. Satan had everything, but he wanted more.

Through your widespread trade
> you were filled with violence,
> and you sinned.
So *I drove you in disgrace from the mount of God,*
> and *I expelled you, O guardian cherub,*
> from among the fiery stones.
Your heart became proud
> on account of your beauty,
and you corrupted your wisdom
> because of your splendor.

So *I threw you to the earth;*

    I made a spectacle of you before kings.

By your many sins and dishonest trade

    you have desecrated your sanctuaries. (28:16-18)

Perhaps the final lines in this prophecy against "the king of Tyre" look far into the future, to foretell Satan's end when he's thrown into the lake of fire (Revelation 20:10) and disappears forever from the sight of man or angel:

So *I made a fire come out from you,*

    and it consumed you,

and *I reduced you to ashes* on the ground

    in the sight of all who were watching.

All the nations who knew you

    are appalled at you;

you have come to a horrible end

    and will be no more. (28:18-19)

As a glimpse of Satan, which seems a likely interpretation, this passage is clear that he was not created evil. As John Calvin says, "everything damnable in him he brought upon himself, by his revolt and fall." All things in their original nature were created good, including Satan. But Satan chose to follow himself instead of following God, and so "corrupted" his "wisdom" (Ezekiel 28:17). Satan no longer speaks God's language, but has brought forth his own, as Jesus tells us: "When he lies, he speaks *his native language,* for he is a liar and the father of lies" (John 8:44).

Satan's Inner Rebellion

Isaiah 14 looks deeper into the nature of Satan's rebellion.

The passage opens this way: "O *morning star,* son of the dawn!" (14:12), or as the King James Version styles it, "O *Lucifer,* son of the morning"

("Lucifer" comes from a name meaning "light-bearer" that was used in Latin translations of this verse; we'll go ahead and use this traditional name here). This brilliant one being addressed here was the Satan "before."

But now this "taunt" (14:4) aimed at Lucifer begins,

> How *you have fallen from heaven*...!
> You have been cast down to the earth,
>> you who once laid low the nations! (14:12)

What follows is Lucifer's declaration of independence. Notice the five vows he speaks in his heart—five promises Lucifer makes to himself, each one beginning with the words "I will":

> You said in your heart,
>> "*I will* ascend to heaven;
> *I will* raise my throne
>> above the stars of God;
> *I will* sit enthroned on the mount of assembly,
>> on the utmost heights of the sacred mountain.
> *I will* ascend above the tops of the clouds;
>> *I will* make myself like the Most High." (14:13-14)

Lucifer first of all wanted God's *place*. He said, "I will ascend *to heaven*," apparently referring to the highest and holiest heaven where God alone resides, a place even higher than where the angels dwell. (Remember that Paul speaks in 2 Corinthians 12:2 of three heavens.) Lucifer wanted to replace God at the pinnacle of everything. He wanted to be "enthroned... on the utmost heights of the sacred mountain," and to "ascend above the tops of the clouds." Both of these last phrases speak of the places of God's presence.

Second, Lucifer wanted God's *position* and *authority*. He said, "I will raise *my throne above the stars of God*," and "I will sit *enthroned* on the mount of assembly." The "stars" and the "assembly" here are most likely references to the other angels. Lucifer wanted sole prominence and power over all of them.

Third, Lucifer was determined to take God's *likeness*. "I will make myself like the Most High." He wanted God's privileges, his independence, his worship.

How utterly unlike God he was in this! Just look at the stark contrast between Lucifer's words and the attitude of Christ:

> Who, being *in very nature God*,
>> did not consider equality with God something to be grasped,
>
> but *made himself nothing*,
>> taking the very nature of a servant,
>> being made in human likeness. (Philippians 2:6-7)

Lucifer's sin above all was pride. And pride goes before destruction, as Isaiah goes on to show:

> But you are brought down to the grave,
>> to the depths of the pit. (14:15)

Lucifer's pride turned an angel into a devil. His self-originated pride brought God's curse upon him. The devil became the sworn enemy of humility.

How could Satan's story have happened? How could such a plunge into ruin come about for someone who was "the model of perfection"?

We know the answer is pride. But when God created Lucifer, didn't he know that pride would captivate this angel's heart?

Yes, we must conclude, since God is all-knowing, he had to have known this.

But could God have prevented it?

Yes, God is all-powerful. He surely could have prevented Satan's fall.

Why didn't he then?

The answer seems to lie in the mystery that Lucifer was created with freedom to choose his course, just as we are. Lucifer used his gift against the Giver. And God "respected" his choice, just as he respects ours.

Lessons from Satan's Fall

What can we learn from Satan's fall?

First of all, recognize the power of pride. I don't believe any temptations face us more frequently or confront us more persistently or entice us more subtly than the temptation to pride. I heard it said this way: "The devil sleeps like an animal in the shadow of good works, waiting for us to conceive a secret admiration of ourselves."

How much are you secretly admiring yourself these days? You're surely more like Satan in those moments than while doing any other sin you could think of.

Satan's game plan is the strategy of pride. It's the approach he's used down through history and still uses today. I suppose he hasn't had a fresh idea since the day he started; he just keeps repackaging the old stuff over and over again. And men keep falling for it. His method *works*. We're as willing to be flattered by ourselves as by others.

But "God opposes the proud" (James 4:6, 1 Peter 5:5). If he so quickly and thoroughly opposed a perfect and glorious angel who became prideful, God can certainly put the brakes on any of the rest of us as well. How much of our spiritual ineffectiveness is related directly to pride?

Satanic activity in all its raw, deceptive form is at work even among God's people. He is the "enemy" who comes and sows weeds among the wheat (Matthew 13:24-30). The "I wills" of Satan still rear their heads today throughout our congregations. It's like a virus—little pockets of pride and discontent that become power pockets, growing like cancer.

Satan will get a church any way he can, and pride has proven the surest and quickest way.

Second, stay alert to Satan's purposes and plans. Having fallen himself, Satan went back to Eden to trigger the fall of mankind. Just as he brought unspeakable tragedy to Adam and Eve through his seductive skill, so he continues to carry out his deceitful program against angels and humanity. He wants to destroy us and render us useless to the kingdom of God. He's on an all-out mission to populate hell with non-Christians, including all your neighbors and friends and family members who have not yet received Christ. He wants to take with him into the fire as many "good" people as we'll let him have. He's delighted when those who still reject Christ as Savior are kept firmly in his grip by our failure to pray for them and witness to them.

Satan's legacy is everywhere. Every sinner and every sin is a mark to his credit. "He who does what is sinful is *of the devil*" (1 John 3:8). Jesus calls him not only "a liar" but also "the *father* of lies" (John 8:44), because every lie was ultimately born in his mouth.

That's why in the same verse Jesus told his unbelieving listeners, "You belong to *your father,* the devil." Sin is the image of Satan in those who have not been reborn as children of God. All of us are growing either in likeness to God or in likeness to the devil.

We can't afford to be asleep to Satan's strategy and tactics. Notice how Scripture's insights into his schemes and character make us instantly want to be on our guard. Notice precisely what these passages say that Satan *does:*

"Your enemy the devil *prowls around* like a roaring lion *looking for someone to devour*" (1 Peter 5:8).

He's "a strong man, fully armed," who *"guards* his own house" so that "his possessions are safe" (Luke 11:21).

He's "the ruler of the kingdom of the air, the spirit who is *now at work* in those who are disobedient" (Ephesians 2:2).

He's "the god of this age" who "has *blinded* the minds of unbelievers" (2 Corinthians 4:4).

"He was a *murderer* from the beginning, not holding to the truth, for there is no truth in him. When he *lies,* he speaks his native language, for he is *a liar* and the father of lies" (John 8:44).

He has this world in his grip. "We know ... that the whole world is *under the control* of the evil one" (1 John 5:19).

And what's most galling of all is that this prowling, roaring, hungry, strong, greedy, active, blinding, murdering, controlling deceiver actually "masquerades as an angel of *light*" (2 Corinthians 11:14).

"The object of all these descriptions," writes Calvin,

> is to make us more cautious and vigilant, and more prepared for the contest.... Wherefore let this be the use to which we turn all these statements.

Even his names spell trouble. The word *Satan* means "accuser." *Devil* means "slanderer." He's called "the dragon, that ancient serpent" (Revelation 20:2), and "the tempter" (Matthew 4:3, 1 Thessalonians 3:5). His designations are "Beelzebub" (Matthew 10:25), meaning "lord of flies," and "Belial" (2 Corinthians 6:15), meaning "worthlessness" or "ruin."

Satan is not God's equal, but he is God's sworn enemy. His tactic with Eve in Eden was to discredit God, and this is still his procedure today. Do you care at all for the honor and glory of God? Do you have allegiance to God's kingdom? Then you must make God's enemy yours.

If the name *Christian* means anything to you, you have no choice but to resist the enemy of Christ, for "the reason the Son of God appeared was to destroy the devil's work" (1 John 3:8). Jesus calls him "the prince of this world" (John 12:31), but adds, "he has *no hold on me*" (14:30). "The prince of this world *now stands condemned*" (16:11). Through his own death and resurrection, Christ has already made Satan's defeat certain. The war is won. But all the battles have not yet been played out. Will you accept the privilege of being a soldier in these victories?

That leads to the third lesson: Remember the supremacy and preeminence of God. Satan did not get away with his pride. And he's not getting away with anything now. He is free on earth to do his damage only to the extent of the length of his chain, and God himself has chained him. The devil cannot go beyond God's permission. He cannot do anything against God's will and God's consent.

It's indeed a mystery. In one place Calvin comments this way on Satan's object and options:

> He eagerly and of set purpose opposes God, aiming at those things which he deems most contrary to the will of God. *But as God holds him bound and fettered by the curb of his power,* he executes those things only for which permission has been given him, and thus, however unwilling, obeys his Creator, being forced... to do Him service.

In Scripture we see this not only in the sweeping epic of Job, where Satan was able to batter the man only after God said, "He is in your hands" (1:12, 2:6), but also elsewhere. For example, an evil spirit tormented King Saul, but it is called "an evil spirit *from the Lord*" (1 Samuel 16:14, 19:9) because God allowed it.

Even Paul encountered this. A "messenger from Satan" came to torment him (2 Corinthians 12:7), but Paul deeply understood God's perspective. He didn't wrangle against Satan, but "pleaded with the Lord to take it away from me" (12:8), since he knew the Lord had sent it. Paul also discovered God's purpose in allowing the tormentor's visit: "to keep me from becoming conceited" (12:7).

It's true that Satan can be a controlling power even in the lives of believers who aren't depending on God. But even when Satan "has taken them captive to do his will," God still offers the hope and method for "escape from the trap of the devil" (2 Timothy 2:25). There's always "a way out" (1 Corinthians 10:13), especially for those who keep in mind the big picture and the final score: "The God of peace will soon crush Satan under your feet" (Romans 16:20).

For the time being, as part of Christ's body we feel the sting when Satan "strikes his heel"; but we'll also share in the retaliation when Christ "crushes his head" (Genesis 3:15).

Satan's Hosts

Satan is not alone in his spiritual attacks.

Jesus speaks of the eternal fire prepared "for the devil *and his angels*" (Matthew 25:41). Satan *"and his angels"* are referred to together in Revelation 12:9. In Matthew 12:24 he is called "Beelzebub, the prince *of demons.*"

We have more than one enemy confronting us, and it's possible we may be attacked by more than one simultaneously. It was said of Mary Magdalene that Jesus drove "seven demons" out of her (Mark 16:9, Luke 8:2). One unfortunate man had been besieged by an entire *legion* of demons (Mark 5:9-15, Luke 8:30-33).

These spirits are rational beings, not diseases or ailments, or tricks of the imagination. They possess all the attributes of personality. They even believe in God, as James tells us: "You believe that there is one God. Good! Even *the demons believe* that — and shudder" (2:19). Demons think and believe and hear and speak.

Who are they, and where did they come from?

Satan himself could not have created them, because only God is the Creator. The best explanation is that they are fallen angels who at some point in time joined in Satan's rebellion.

Peter tells us:

> God did not spare *angels* when they sinned, but sent them to hell, putting them into gloomy dungeons to be held for judgment.... (2 Peter 2:4)

Jude speaks of "the *angels* who did not keep their positions of authority but abandoned their own home" (Jude 6).

One passage hints at the possibility that as many as a third of the angels in heaven fell when Satan did. In the book of Revelation, John saw "an enormous red dragon" whose tail "swept *a third of the stars* out of the sky and flung them to the earth" (12:3-4). The dragon is identified as Satan later in this chapter. And stars, as we've learned, frequently represent angels both in Revelation and elsewhere. The vision John saw here may well have been a playback of what happened in heaven before human history began.

Spiritual Warfare

Demons are Satan's servants, and are committed to his scheme to thwart the plan of God. Often in Scripture they are also called "evil spirits" or "unclean spirits." They are ruled by Satan himself, and they share in his dirty work.

With enemies like these, we need friends. God has provided them, and shows them to us in his Word.

Lock on to the fact that nothing demons do can be outside God's good purpose and designs. Never forget this: "Neither angels *nor demons…nor any powers…*nor anything else in all creation, will be able to separate us from the love of God that is in Christ Jesus our Lord" (Romans 8:38-39).

Calvin once more supplies a good picture. He shows us God "turning the unclean spirits hither and thither at his pleasure," all with the intention of "exercising believers." The demons are always "warring against them, assailing them with wiles, urging them with solicitations, pressing close upon them, disturbing, alarming, and occasionally wounding, but *never conquering or oppressing them.*"

Just as Satan and the demons share a common origin and a common passion and work, so they also must face a common fate. Paul assures us that Jesus "must reign until he has put *all his enemies* under his feet" (1 Corinthians 15:25). That includes the devil and every demon.

In every encounter between Jesus and demons in the Gospels, Jesus was the overcomer. His followers share in that power. When Christ's disciples returned "with joy" from a ministry trip, they reported to Jesus, "Lord, even *the demons submit to us* in your name" (Luke 10:17). And Jesus answered, *"I saw Satan fall* like lightning from heaven."

Jude says that God has kept the fallen angels "in darkness, *bound with everlasting chains* for judgment on the great Day" (Jude 6).

Meanwhile, until that great Day, we wrestle. We *"struggle . . .* against the powers of this dark world and against the spiritual forces of evil in the heavenly realms" (Ephesians 6:12).

In this struggle there is someone who shows us how to endure and how to win, someone whose life knew both spiritual warfare and the touch of angels more than anyone who ever walked the earth.

As you can feel with your fingers, the remaining pages in this book are few. Only a short while and a short space are left to devote to the topic of angels before our study here must come to an end. Together let's bring it to a close by spending that short while with this Someone whom angels have known so well.

Chapter Fourteen

THE ANGELS
AND JESUS

H E WAS "seen by angels," we're told in a short, sweet line of what sounds like a hymn Paul shares with us in 1 Timothy 3:16. Jesus left heaven, the home of spirits, and came to earth, the home of flesh.

And angels watched in wonder.

Oh, look: One of those angels who watched in wonder has just joined us. It's our old friend, the guide who took us earlier on all those fast trips through Scripture to watch the goings-on of angels.

We welcome him back, and thank him for the note he left us.

He asks if we'd like to travel back into the past again. We eagerly agree.

He says that this time we'll spend our entire journey within the span of one man's earthly lifetime. "This is one man's story," our guide tells us. "It's my *favorite* story," he adds. "And yours too."

We understand. And we're glad, because we're always finding something new in that story. What will we discover this time?

"Let's go," he says. And we're off.

At His Birth

Grassy hills, near a village, at night. We see shepherds cloaked in camel-hair coats, huddled around a campfire. We know where we are in terms of both geography and history: close to Bethlehem, two thousand years ago.

"By man's measure," says our guide, "it's been hundreds of years since we messengers appeared on earth with great openness. But a new day has arrived. Only months ago Gabriel came and spoke to Zechariah and then to Mary. Another of my brothers revealed himself to Joseph in a dream.

"Yes, in these days the world will see us more at work here. People will also notice more miracles of God. And our enemies the demons will be more exposed as well."

In the dark stillness on the hillside, we reflect on his words.

Suddenly the shepherds throw themselves to the ground, stricken in terror by a blinding light. We knew it was coming, but we're startled too.

The angel reassures the shaking shepherds, then speaks his news: "Today a Savior has been born *to you.*..."

Our guide whispers. "Did you hear that? The Savior didn't come here for angels. He came for those shepherds, and for you, and for others like you."

Again he looks out across the hillside. We see the reflection of starlight and angel-light dancing in his eyes.

"And we're *glad* for you!" he shouts, just as the sky becomes jam-packed with countless angels. They all have that same look of ecstasy on their faces.

"GLORY TO GOD IN THE HIGHEST!" they exclaim. They're looking up.

Our guide happily explains. "They're exalting God, and telling all the rest of the angels they left behind to join in the praise as well. The sky here above this pasture could never hold all of us."

You and I can't get over the joy of all these messengers. The news they're announcing has nothing to do with them, really. But they're as happy about it as if they too had just been snatched from the clutches of hell. We decide it must be because they simply adore Jesus so much.

After all, up in heaven they've already been with him for ages and ages. They must know him so well, and love him so deeply. And since *he* was so glad to be coming here now, they can be glad with him.

THE ANGELS AND JESUS 219

At His Temptation

The volume fades on the angel chorus. So does the picture. Another scene fades in: brown, barren hills of the Judean wilderness. A man—the Son of Man—is on one hillside, but not alone. The dark form of the tempter is there too. Just a glimpse of him is all we can handle. We avert our eyes and wonder how Jesus can endure Satan's ugliness.

Again our guide explains: "In this encounter, the enemy need not clothe himself in light, as he does so often to deceive your kind. He knows that no disguise can veil his nature from the Son of God."

We keep our heads turned away, but we listen. Satan's words sound like garbled noise to us. But we can understand Jesus clearly. His strong voice keeps quoting Scripture, calmly and triumphantly. We fear and loathe this creature before him who dares to tempt him. Somehow, though, it makes us treasure every line Jesus speaks:

> *It is written:* "Man does not live on bread alone, but on every word that comes from the mouth of God."
> *It is written:* "Do not put the Lord your God to the test."
> *It is written:* "Worship the Lord your God, and serve him only."

We know that we, too, will be facing the tempter again. So we won't forget these counter-attack words from Jesus.

When we turn around, the tempter is gone. The battle is over.

Already angels are at Jesus' side and at his feet, to strengthen and nourish him.

"The Scriptures have told you," says our guide, "that the Son of Man for a little while was made lower than the angels. These years of his life on earth make up that 'little while.' During this window of time, my brothers and I can serve the Lord here in ways we never could in heaven.

"Long ago my fellow servants and I ministered to God's people Israel in the wilderness. Now Jesus is in the wilderness. We will minister to him as well."

In Gethsemane

We move to a different scene, but one where our guide has taken us before: an olive grove, with Jesus bent over in agony in Gethsemane.

A flicker of a memory enters our consciousness. Suddenly we remember the heart of Lucifer hammering away defiantly, *"I will... I will... I will... I will... I will...."* We shake off that distasteful thought, and focus our minds again on the praying Christ.

"Not my will," he cries with clean, pure earnestness, "but yours be done."

He pauses in his praying. Everything is so quiet. An angel appears at his side, wiping the sweat from his brow and temples.

With teary eyes our guide says, "None of us had ever done that before, until the 'little while' came. And now, the end approaches."

Before our eyes the scene rapidly advances. The disciples, who had been sleeping a stone's throw away, are awake and standing.

A mob of soldiers and others has entered the olive grove. They've come to arrest Jesus.

We look around. The angel is gone. But Jesus says to the tense crowd around him, "Do you think I cannot call on my Father, and he will at once put at my disposal more than twelve legions of angels?"

Our guide nods. "He's right," he tells us.

After His Resurrection

The night is over. Dawn is here—the beginning of a bright Jerusalem morning. We're in another garden in another section of the city.

We see soldiers, tired from a long, uneventful night, standing guard at a hillside tomb. You and I remember reading about this in the last chapter of Matthew.

Suddenly the ground is shaking. An angel appears out of nowhere, coming as fast as a lightning bolt and just as bright.

The soldiers are as good as dead. Trembling and pale, they flee.

The angel moves a massive stone that covers the mouth of the tomb. He rolls it aside effortlessly, then calmly sits down on top of it.

"My brother there—he's very strong," our guide tells us. "I know him well."

We step close enough to look inside the tomb. It's empty. Grave clothes are neatly folded on the low stone shelf where a corpse should be lying.

Now the sun is rising.

Two women walk hesitantly into the garden, staring from a distance at the tomb. The closer they get, the more worried they look.

The angel stays seated. We get the feeling that if he stood or made any move at all, those two women would be out of here faster than you could say Pontius Pilate.

We hear the angel clear his throat. He's about to say something.

Our guide leans over and tells us quietly, "He's so excited about this assignment he can hardly stand it. I know him well."

The angel's voice is calm and confident: "Do not be afraid," he says to the women. Instead of turning and running, they stand and listen.

He continues: "I know you seek *Jesus*, who was crucified. He is not here. He has risen!—*just as he said.*"

Our guide whispers to us again: "He relishes every word of this. I know him well."

The angel sweeps his arm wide toward the tomb's open door and says, "Come, see the place where he lay." The women cautiously peek in. Their faces look dazed. The truth is slowly sinking in.

"Go quickly!" the angel commands. His voice grows bolder with every phrase: "Tell his disciples: 'He has risen from the dead and is going ahead of you into Galilee. There you will see him.'"

A smile takes over his face, and he adds triumphantly:

"*Now* I have told you."

Our Conclusion

This last scene fades.

Our guide puts forth the same question he asked us in our earlier trip: "What have you learned?"

After a pause, you decide to answer for both of us:

"That angels truly love the Lord, and will always love to serve him...

and so will I."

SOURCE NOTES

Thomas Aquinas, *Summa Theologica* (1267-1273).

John Calvin, *Institutes of the Christian Religion* (1536-1559; translated by Henry Beveridge, 1845-1846).

Lewis Sperry Chafer, *Major Bible Themes* (Durham Publishing, 1926).

Christianity Today: Timothy Jones, "Rumors of Angels" (April 5, 1993).

Douglas Connelly, *Angels Around Us* (Intervarsity Press, 1994).

W. A. Criswell, *Expository Sermons on Revelation* (Zondervan Publishing, 1962).

C. Fred Dickason, *Angels Elect and Evil* (Moody Press, 1975).

Millard J. Erickson, *Christian Theology* (Baker Book House, 1983-1985).

Expositors Bible Commentary (Zondervan Publishing, 1976-1992).

A. C. Gaebelein, *The Angels of God* (Baker Book House, 1969).

Billy Graham, *Angels: God's Secret Agents* (Word Publishing, 1975).

Matthew Henry, *Commentary on the Bible* (1704-1721).

John Phillips and Jerry Vines, *Exploring Daniel* (Loizeaux Brothers, 1990).

Hope Price, *Angels* (Macmillan Publishing [London], 1993).

Corrie ten Boom, *A Prisoner — And Yet* (Evangelical Publishers [Toronto], 1947).

Henry Clarence Thiessen, *Lectures in Systematic Theology* (Eerdmans Publishing, 1949).

Time: Nancy Gibbs, "Angels Among Us" (December 27, 1993).

A. W. Tozer, *The Pursuit of God* (Christian Publications, 1948); *The Divine Conquest* (Christian Publications, 1950); *The Knowledge of the Holy* (Harper Collins, 1961).

J. M. Wilson, "Angel," in *International Standard Bible Encyclopedia* (Eerdmans Publishing, 1915, 1979).

SCRIPTURE INDEX

SUBJECT INDEX

O Lord Almighty
(O Lord of Hosts,
O God of Heaven's Angelic Armies),
blessed is the man
who trusts in you.

Psalm 84:12

Other books by Dr. David Jeremiah

The Prayer Matrix

Prayer: The Great Adventure

The Joy of Encouragement